"Good teach(
see so clearly that ....
The authors, Vanderbilt Brabson III and Frederick Brabson Sr. teach like Jesus the Master Teacher taught by employing illustrations to turn the windows of life's experiences into mirrors for self-identification.

"This book is a photo album in which readers can see themselves, use the images to diagnose their predicaments, and more importantly, find redemptive, active, and life-changing prescriptions within the personhood of Jesus Christ. *If the Shoe Fits* is theology in practical and identifiable illustrations, not just in sermonic propositions. This book will be a profitable addition to the library of any serious student of Scripture—whether one stands in the pulpit or classroom or sits in the quietude of home."
—*Dr. Robert Smith Jr.*
Charles T. Carter Baptist Chair of Divinity
Beeson Divinity School, Samford University

"*If the Shoe Fits* is everything advertised and more! I've long believed that biblical preaching is comprised of the solid exposition of scripture that is illustrated clearly with a call to application. The authors have provided a treasure chest full of illustrations and applications of biblical truth in their book *If the Shoe Fits*. I am honored to endorse this practical book for every pastor who desires to communicate more clearly and every Christ follower who wants to live in more victory."
—*Randy C. Davis*
President & Executive Director
Tennessee Baptist Mission Board

"*If the Shoe Fits* is refreshing and insightful into the truth of God's word. The illustrations are real life and timely. I found the stories a real delight while at the same time driving home important truths of the Word being understood from the unique perspective of a powerful story. I highly recommend this to anyone who preaches and teaches God's word. There is nothing as powerful as a good illustration. This book is full of them. You will definitely enjoy this book."
—*Jay Wells*
Former Director, Black Development
LifeWay Christian Resources

IF THE  FITS

Spiritual Truths Illustrated
in Great Stories

Vanderbilt Brabson III
and Frederick E. Brabson Sr.

Knoxville TN

If the Shoe Fits
by Vanderbilt Brabson III and Frederick E. Brabson Sr.
Copyright ©2019 Vanderbilt Brabson III and Frederick E. Brabson Sr.

All rights reserved. This book is protected under the copyright laws of the United States of America. This book may not be copied or reprinted for commercial gain or profit.

Unless otherwise identified, Scriptures are taken from the King James Version of the Bible. Public domain.

Scriptures marked NASB are taken from the *New American Standard Bible*, Copyright ©1960, 1962, 1963, 1968, 1971, 1973, 1975, 1977 by The Lockman Foundation.

Scriptures marked MSG are taken from *THE MESSAGE*. Copyright © by Eugene H. Peterson 1993, 1994, 1995, 1996, 2000, 2002. Used by permission of NavPress Publishing Group.

ISBN 978-0-9828427-6-8
For Worldwide Distribution
Printed in the U.S.A.

> Doretha Publishing
> P.O. Box 566
> Knoxville, TN 37901

Table of Contents

Foreword   *ix*

Preface   *xi*

1. The Scorpion and the Frog   *1*
The warring of two natures within each Christian

2. A Boy, a Vase, and a Piece of Candy   *5*
The consequences of our obedience and disobedience

3. A Man and a Cow   *9*
Having the right priorities and putting God first

4. A Lad, a Barn Rooftop, and a Rusty Nail   *13*
Discerning God's hand in our circumstances

5. A Young Lady, a Pastor, and a Dance Floor   *17*
Our willingness to sacrifice our rights for Jesus Christ

6. A Professor, a Student, and a Bible   *24*
A nonbeliever's inability to truly understand the word of God

7. Seeing God   *30*
Seeing what we choose to see

8. A Young Lady Witnessing in the Park   *35*
Persecution for our faith in Jesus Christ

9. Excuses   *42*
Excuses we make to avoid right actions

10. A Lady and Her Revenge   *47*
Unforgiveness makes slaves of us

11. One and Forty-Nine   *54*
The pitfalls of succumbing to peer pressure

12. Reasoning with the Unreasonable   *58*
The challenges of sharing spiritual truths with the unredeemed

13. The Bigger They Come, the Harder They Fall   *66*
The perils of pride

14. Senior Citizens and a Joy Ride   *71*
Becoming indifferent to the things of God

15. A Pardon from the King   *76*
The consequences of never acknowledging any responsibility

16. Empty Promises   *82*
When our spiritual talking and walking do not align

17. An Appointed Time   *85*
Our inescapable appointment with death

18. A Hiker, a Ledge, and a Voice   *90*
Letting fear stand in the way of our faith

19. Remembering to Love   *96*
The temptation to be self-righteous

20. A Broken Will   *103*
The pain and discomfort of resisting God's will

21. A Father, A Son, and an Issue of Discipline   *108*
The chastening hand of God

22. A Sign, a Warning, and the Undiscerning   *115*
God's warning signs we tend to ignore

23. More, Lord, More   *122*
A lack of appreciation and acknowledgment of God's blessings

24. Skin on His Promises   *127*
Ambassadors for Jesus Christ

25. Falling and Failure   *134*
An issue of carnality

26. A Lad and His Model Plane   *139*
Redeeming that which was lost

27. A Boy, a Clock, and an Old Man   *144*
Appreciation of God's grace

28. A Friend on Whom You Can Depend   *149*
What a friend we have in Jesus

29. A Question of Compassion   *155*
The absolute importance of compassion for others

30. Strawberries and Squash   *160*
God's ability to take the bad and work it for our good and His glory

*This book is dedicated to the countless ministers
and Bible teachers who, over the years,
have shared these and/or similar stories
in hopes of strengthening the faithful
and reaching their audiences for Jesus Christ.
To God alone be the glory.*

Foreword

In our household growing up, I was the third of five children being raised by a single mother. Our dear mother always worked two to three jobs to make ends meet, which meant throughout the week we kids typically waved at her as she hurried out the door to one of her jobs.

Not having the luxury to spend a lot of time at home with us, my mom had very few rules for each of us kids to obey. However, there was this one rule every child in our house was required to obey, and it was not open to negotiation. That rule was in regards to Sundays. Every Sunday morning everyone living in her house, drinking her water, sleeping in her beds, and eating her food *had* to attend church. Regarding this one rule, our mother tolerated no exceptions and no excuses! On Sunday afternoons our dear mother would gather each of us into the living room to give us an opportunity as a family to talk about what we had heard in our Sunday School class and in our pastor's sermon.

It was from those Sunday afternoon family meetings that I learned the importance of hearing the stories communicated in a sermon or in a Sunday School lesson. I could not always remember a sermon title or Sunday School topic, but in our Sunday afternoon family meetings I always remembered the stories told by the pastor or the Sunday School teacher—and that was over fifty-five years ago!

Well, that is the beauty of this book that you are about to read: *If the Shoe Fits: Spiritual Truths Illustrated in Great Stories*. My friends, Pastor Frederick E. Brabson Sr. and Vanderbilt Brabson III, have literally saved for every preacher, pastor, Sunday School teacher, evangelist, seminary student, and Bible study teacher the precious time it requires to search out and find just the right story to communicate and illustrate the truths of their message. In this book the authors are doing for us what Jesus did during His earthly ministry when He taught His audiences by the use of parables. No matter who His audience was, Jesus utilized parables to illustrate the spiritual lessons He was conveying.

This short, easy reading book has thirty stories covering a range of subjects that will leave your audience requesting, "Please, tell us another story!" That's how I felt when I got to the last chapter of this enjoyable book. I wanted to say, "Please, tell me another story!" My only regret is that I wish I had a book like this in my library years ago. I know it would have helped in trying to illustrate difficult passages in my preaching and teaching throughout the years.

I encourage you to read this book, apply this book, but most of all, tell others about this book so that they too may be blessed as I have been. Thanks Pastor Brabson and Vanderbilt Brabson III for *If the Shoe Fits*, a book that will help all who read it.

—*Fred Luter Jr.*

Pastor, Franklin Avenue Baptist Church, New Orleans, LA,
Past President of the Southern Baptist Convention

Preface

Every day across this nation and around the world, thousands of pastors, evangelists, Bible teachers, Christian parents, as well as other Christians—both men and women, young and old wrestle with the same recurring dilemma—how to skillfully take the most profound spiritual truths and communicate them to our families, our friends, and our wider audiences in the simplest way possible that will facilitate understanding and retention.

So what should you and I do when we need the perfect story to illustrate the spiritual truth we are seeking to convey? The answer is we can turn to our bookshelves and thumb through *If the Shoe Fits*.

If a picture is worth a thousand words, then a good story is certainly worth the valuable lesson it teaches. Someone once said, "If you take a lickin', it ought to teach you a lesson. But if you look back and only remember the lickin', you didn't learn the lesson." Allegories are like that. Sometimes the most profound truths can be mined from the shallow depths of a simple story. Some stories paint a picture as big as life itself on the canvas of our mind. And when we get the picture, we learn the lesson.

When Jesus spoke to fishermen, to get His point across, He talked about making them fishers of men. To farmers He talked about sowing seeds. To shepherds He talked about sheep and told them He is the Good Shepherd who gives His life for the sheep. By addressing these groups in this way, Jesus used one of the most effective methods of teaching there is—the use of parables. Through parables Jesus spoke of those physical things familiar to His audience to facilitate their understanding of those spiritual things that were unfamiliar to them.

Around the world, eager listeners sit patiently at the feet of countless pastors, evangelists, Bible teachers, and parents expounding biblical doctrines and spiritual truths. Unfortunately for most of us, we forget a lot more than we retain. Few listeners, however, forget a good story.

If the Shoe Fits is all about learning valuable lessons through pictures painted by those who use modern day parables in their teaching. Every lesson taught using this collection of narratives gives the reader invaluable spiritual insight for daily Christian living. *If the Shoe Fits* is an excellent resource for pastors, evangelists, Bible teachers, conference speakers, seminary students, parents, and anyone who desires to retain and/or share valuable, spiritual lessons packaged in a simple story.

Whether we are struggling to find the perfect anecdote to drive home a sermon's theme or Bible lesson, or simply to share spiritual truth with a family member or friend, we will find both humor and inspiration in these pages.

In this day of information overload, nothing is more frustrating than knowing deep within ourselves that most of the spiritual truths we hear, learn, and share with others will not be remembered within the next twenty-four to forty-eight hours. However, we all can agree that when we hear a good story, we tend to remember the spiritual message conveyed by that particular story.

Most of us as Christians, if not all of us, are always seeking to receive and impart greater understanding and retention of spiritual truths. Humorous and inspirational stories accomplish that by evoking an emotional response in its listeners—such as laughter, sadness, and compassion—to name a few.

Since any good story, such as those found in the pages of this book, has more than one possible application, we pray that the stories contained within will prove to be an invaluable resource to you for years to come.

1

The Scorpion and the Frog

An old scorpion became marooned on a deserted island without any food. The only other living creature on the island was an old frog who decided it would swim to the mainland as opposed to remaining on the island and starving to death.

Realizing his dilemma, the old scorpion approached the frog by the water's edge and reasoned, "Look, it's about one mile to the mainland, and you could swim there easily with me on your back."

"Are you kidding me?" the old frog said. "As soon as you get me out there in the middle of that ocean, you'll sting me!"

"Don't be ridiculous," argued the scorpion. "Surely you can see why I want off this island. There's no food. If I stay here, I'll surely die!" The old scorpion broke down and began to weep.

Moved by the old scorpion's tears, the old frog finally acquiesced to the scorpion's request.

"Oh, you won't regret this Mr. Frog! I'll be really good!" pledged the old scorpion.

So the scorpion climbed aboard the frog's back and away the frog swam. When the two were about a half mile out into the ocean, suddenly that old scorpion wound up his tail and buried his stinger deep into the old frog's back, mortally wounding him.

In great pain and anguish the old, dying frog looked up as he slowly began to sink. "Why—why'd you go and do a thing like that? Don't you realize that now we're both going to die?"

Terrified, the old scorpion shouted, "I know, Mr. Frog! I know! I really tried with all my might not to sting you, but I just couldn't help myself. You see, it's my nature."

Although that old scorpion knew that stinging the frog meant his own demise, he still had no power to act contrary to his true nature.

And so it is with us as well. A thief is not a thief because he steals. He steals because he is a thief. A liar is not a liar because he lies. He lies because he is a liar. And a sinner is not a sinner because he/she sins. He/she sins because he/she is a sinner—which is the nature with which we were all born.

Walking and living a sinful lifestyle comes naturally for us when we have not come to a saving knowledge of Jesus Christ. If as a non-Christian I desire to live my life in service to God, apart from a genuine relationship with Jesus Christ, I will soon discover on a daily basis that the power to live such a life is simply not present within me.

In his second letter to Timothy, Paul warned the young overseer to be on guard for individuals who publicly make a show of religion while at the same time their daily conduct reveals their true, unregenerate nature.

This know also, that in the last days perilous times shall come. For men shall be lovers of their own selves, covetous, boasters, proud, blasphemers, disobedient to parents, unthankful, unholy, without natural affection, trucebreakers, false accusers, incontinent, fierce, despisers of those that are good, traitors, heady, highminded, lovers of pleasures more than lovers of God; having a form of godliness but denying the power thereof: from such turn away (2 Timothy 3:1-5).

Paul declared that such individuals have an outward form of godliness but lack the abiding presence and power of the Holy Spirit within to truly live for Jesus Christ.

A popular doctrinal statement taught in many of our seminaries reads,

> "No degree of reformation, however great; no attainment of morality, however high; no culture, however attractive; no baptism or ordinance, however administered will bring a sinner one step closer to salvation in God than what is already provided for in the shed blood and substitutionary death of Jesus Christ."

Only through the salvation brought about in a genuine relationship with Jesus Christ will an individual find freedom from their bondage to their old sin nature (Romans 6:6) and the power to truly live as God's child (John 1:12).

What about us today? Are we one of those individuals who simply attempts to appear godly? Even if we attend church regularly, use Christian clichés, and know Christian doctrine but lack a personal, saving knowledge and relationship with Jesus Christ, we will still not possess any real power in our lives to truly live for God daily.

> "It is not my ability, but my response to God's ability, that counts." —*Corrie ten Boom*

Corrie ten Boom was a Christian Holocaust survivor

who helped a number of Jews escape the Nazis during World War II.

If this story describes where you are spiritually—a slave to your old nature and lacking a genuine relationship with Jesus Christ, please pray the following:

Dear heavenly Father, I have come to realize that my attempt to serve You, apart from a genuine relationship with Your Son Jesus Christ, is at best futile.

Revelation 3:20 tells me that Jesus is knocking at the door of my heart and asking permission to enter. I hear His voice, and I am now inviting Him into my heart and life to be both my Savior and Lord. I believe that He died for my sins and rose for my justification. Please take that same power You used to raise Jesus' dead body from the grave and use it in my life to make me into a new creature with a new nature in Jesus Christ. Thank You for hearing my prayer. Thank You for forgiving me of my sin, and thank You for accepting me as a child of God through the shed blood and sacrifice of Jesus Christ at Calvary. In Jesus' name I pray. Amen.

2

A Boy, a Vase, and a Piece of Candy

A mother cleverly kept candy out of the reach of her children inside a narrow-necked vase set on a shelf out of their reach. Whenever she wanted to reward one of the children, she would simply turn the vase upside down and out would drop a piece of candy.

She periodically warned the children not to tamper with the vase. One evening, however, while she was in another room, Timmy, her mischievous little son, grabbed a chair to stand on, pulled it across the floor to the shelf, and plunged his little hand down into the neck of that vase. He immediately filled his hand with candy, but because his hand was full, he was unable to withdraw it through the narrow neck of the vase.

Timmy struggled desperately to free himself, but his attempts were futile as long as he continued to hold onto the candy. Having heard the chair scraping across the floor and the rattling of the vase, his mother hurried to the kitchen where she caught her son with his hand still trapped in the vase—all because he refused to release the candy.

All too often Timmy's story describes the plight of us

typical Christians. At the bottom of that vase lies our will. As Christians we desire to experience all the benefits and privileges that come with being a child of God; but despite God's warnings, we tend to want that forbidden candy of having our own way also! And wanting that candy at times leads us to act contrary to what we know to be right in the sight of our loving heavenly Father. When we choose to ignore God's scriptural warnings, experience becomes our teacher; and it can be a very brutal teacher.

Ben Franklin once commented that "Experience is the best school for a fool, for he will learn in no other." Experience will eventually teach us that when we stubbornly hold onto our own will and selfish desires and simultaneously reject God's will for our lives, we inevitably find ourselves imprisoned by the consequences of our actions. Sadly, some of us Christians may find ourselves in bondage to alcohol, pornography, and illicit sex, just to name a few, because of our refusal to heed the teachings and warnings of God in the Holy Scriptures.

It has been said there are three kinds of individuals: Those who make things happen, those who watch things happen, and those who wonder what happened. Actually, there is a fourth kind of individual. There are those who look for the hand of God in what is happening. But to be the latter requires trust—trusting God enough so that we release the forbidden candy and surrender ourselves totally to His will for our lives.

We are encouraged in scripture to have the same attitude and mindset as the Lord Jesus Christ (Philippians 2:5) and to walk even as He walked (1 John 2:6). If we say we are willing to do so, then we should also be willing to pray as Jesus

A Boy, a Vase, and a Piece of Candy

prayed, "…not what I will [heavenly Father], but what Thou wilt" (Mark 14:36).

Catchphrases such as, "If it feels good, do it," "You only go around once in life, so get all the gusto you can," and "Everyone has to decide for themselves what is right for him or her," strongly encourage us to pursue a life void of the truth found in God's Word. Such worldly philosophies seek to persuade us that happiness and freedom wait for us just over the hill or around the corner.

Unfortunately, what truly awaits those who buy into these philosophies is bondage to sin and misery. And the happiness they seek turns out to be an elusive butterfly—somehow always just out of their reach. The source of true happiness, joy, and contentment cannot be found in the forbidden candy of pursuing our own course while ignoring God's will for our lives.

Within each of us is born a God-sized vacuum that God alone is able to fill—an inner hunger that He alone is able to satisfy and an inner thirst that He alone is able to quench. Only when we abandon our will for His will do we discover true happiness, joy, and contentment for our lives as well as the strength we need to truly serve Him.

However, if we choose to disregard God's warnings and insist on pursuing our own course, then God may just simply wait us out and allow trial after trial to take us captive until we are finally exhausted and stripped of all confidence in our own abilities and ingenuity.

> "I have learned to not hold onto things in this life so tightly because it is very painful when God has to pry my fingers loose." —*Corrie ten Boom*

Corrie ten Boom was a Christian Holocaust survivor, who helped a number of Jews escape the Nazis during World War II.

If that happens to be you today, and you have grown weary of resisting God's will for your life and are now ready to surrender to God's very best for you, please pray the following:

Dear heavenly Father, as Jesus prayed, I also pray not my will but Your will be done in every area of my heart and life. Forgive me for pursuing the forbidden candy—that is to say, my own course and my own will. Help me from this moment forward to daily seek Your sovereign will for my life. Please give me an understanding heart and help me to recognize when I am holding onto things of this world too tightly.

Continually remind me that You always know and do those things that are best for me. Also, help me to remember there is a greater purpose and a higher cause to which I have been called as part of Your redemptive plan for this world. Thank You for forgiving me and giving me the desire to please You. I ask these things in Jesus' name. Amen.

3

A Man and A Cow

A man had a cow that gave birth to twin calves. He was so excited he immediately ran back to the house and informed his wife of the great news. In the midst of his excitement, he promised her that he would give one of the calves to the Lord in recognition of God's blessings in their lives.

"Which one?" his wife inquired.

"Oh, it doesn't really matter which one," he answered. "We will just let the two calves grow together, and when they are big enough, the money I get from the sale of the Lord's cow, I will give to the Lord."

A few weeks later a terrible storm arose and lightning struck the man's barn, killing one of the twin calves. After examining the damages, the man returned to the house, met his wife at the door, and sadly informed her, "Aw, honey, I have bad news."

"What is it?" she asked.

"I'm so sorry, but the Lord's calf was killed!" he replied.

Like the farmer in this story, many of us as Christians oftentimes start out with the very best of intentions, but somehow along the way things do not always turn out exactly as we had intended. Facing unexpected, unwanted results sometimes leaves us struggling to keep the spiritual commitments we have previously made.

Take for example our commitment to put God first in our hearts and lives, only to find after an extremely exhausting day, we are too tired to carve out any real quality time for personal devotion. As a result, we put it off—not just that particular evening but again and again.

Ever gotten into bed at night and asked yourself after a few minutes of lying there, "Did I pray tonight?" Or ever caught yourself whispering a prayer of thanksgiving over your food, only to remember in the midst of your prayer you have already asked God's blessings on the food just moments before? I certainly have. Is it possible these things happen to us because our first prayer was no more than a recitation of words? It is as though we unconsciously put our lips in cruise control, disengaged our brains, and allowed our minds to wander elsewhere. Perhaps such things happen to us because we have allowed our thoughts and intentions to become distracted by the things of the world.

Our Lord tells us in His Sermon on the Mount (Matthew 6:33-34) that we are to seek the things of God above everything else in our lives. Jesus said we should not become anxious over what may or may not happen tomorrow because the sovereign God will address those things in our lives when that time comes. If we are not careful, we may find ourselves giving all our time and energy to the temporal things of this world. And if we do, at the end of the day when our energy is spent, we offer up a few quick words to our Lord, knowing He understands our fatigue. Such prayers, like that dead calf, represent the worthless and leftover things we offer to God.

A Man and a Cow

In John 21:15, Jesus asked Peter did he love Him more than these. Some teach that the "these" refers to the other disciples since Peter had previously boasted he was a more devoted follower of Christ than all men, including the other disciples (Matthew 26:33). Others teach that "these" refers to the fish because Peter had told the other disciples he was going back to what was familiar to him—fishing—while he waited on Jesus (John 21:3).

Whether Jesus was referring to the other disciples or the fish is not that important because the application is the same. Jesus wanted Peter to love Him above everything and everyone dear to Peter's heart and become wholly dedicated to his calling—to be a fisher of men (Matthew 4:19).

Jesus is asking each of us that very same question He asked Peter. The question we have to ask ourselves is this: Are we giving greater priority to our possessions, our time, our talents, and our relationships, than we are to the Lordship of Christ in our lives? Hopefully, this question should challenge us to re-evaluate our priorities and determine which things in our lives do we assign the greatest value.

> "If you read history you will find out that the Christians who did most for the present world were precisely those who thought most of the next." —*C.S. Lewis.*

Lewis was an Irish author and scholar. Lewis is known for his work on medieval literature, Christian apologetics, literary criticism, and fiction. He is best known for his children's series, *The Chronicles of Narnia.*

If the Shoe Fits

If you have been guilty of giving other things greater priority than the Lordship of Christ in your life and are now ready to put Him first, please pray the following:

Dear heavenly Father, please be first in my heart and life above everything else. I realize I have not always put You first above all else, but I am willing and need Your help to make it so. Mold me and shape my life into the image of Your beloved Son so that others may see You in me in all that I do. And when life becomes hectic for me, as I know it will at times, and I am tempted to again offer You the worthless and leftover things from my life, please put me in remembrance of my commitment to keep You first above all else. Please provide me with the power to honor this commitment. I ask this in Jesus' name. Amen.

4

A Lad, a Barn Rooftop, and a Rusty Nail

One evening an inquisitive, young lad climbed up to the tin roof of his parent's barn to gaze across the family farm. As he was admiring all the various farm animals and the vast acreages of planted fields, suddenly his foot slipped and he lost his grip, causing him to immediately begin tumbling down the roof to what would be certain death.

Quickly the lad cried out, "Oh God, save me!" and just as the words left his mouth, an old long rusty nail head, protruding through the edge of that roof, suddenly caught one of the lad's trouser straps, bringing the boy to an abrupt stop.

The lad shakily managed to pull himself back up onto the rooftop. As he did, he brushed off his trousers, fixed his strap, looked up toward heaven, and said, "Never mind, Lord, the nail caught me!"

Like the lad in this story, all of us are guilty at times of failing to see the hand of God in our circumstances. There are times when God allows circumstances to totally disrupt our lives, as we see it, in either a positive or negative way. Why so? Perhaps so that He may mold us, shape us, and conform us into the image of His beloved Son Jesus Christ (Romans 8:29). God can take any circumstance in our lives and ultimately make it work to our good and to His glory (Romans 8:28). How? Because with God nothing shall be impossible (Luke 1:37).

We are mere humans, which means God knows that our understanding of the divine and the eternal are limited. Psalms 103:14 reads, "For He knoweth our frame; He remembereth that we are dust." And because we are limited in our understanding, even the best of us at times may find ourselves questioning God, especially during those times when we are experiencing some of life's severest storms. Perhaps some of the hardships we have begged God to remove from our lives are the very things He is allowing and using to accomplish His sovereign will and purpose in us.

There are at least two things of which we can be sure: First, God always knows and understands what He is doing. Secondly, we do not always know and understand what God is doing. We will never know or understand everything. The Lord declared,

For My thoughts are not your thoughts, nor are your ways My ways, says the Lord. For as the heavens are higher than the earth, so are My ways higher than your ways, and My thoughts than your thoughts (Isaiah 55:8-9).

While it is true that adversity in our lives can at times seem devastating, it is also true that how we respond to that adversity can even be more devastating. We either allow adversity to make us bitter, or we allow it to make us better. The difference lies in our ability to see the hand of God in the midst of our circumstances and trust Him to ultimately make

A Lad, a Barn Rooftop, and a Rusty Nail

them work to our good and to His glory. Even during those times when we experience what to us may seem to be insignificant and minor annoyances in our lives, shouldn't we strive to see His hand at work?

The late radio evangelist J. Harold Smith shared with his audience how years ago due to traffic problems, he arrived late at an England airport. Because of his late arrival, the plane took off for the United States without him. Frustrated and annoyed by the incident, Smith had no other choice but to book a later flight. Smith later discovered the plane he was originally scheduled to take back to the states never reached its destination. It developed major engine trouble mid-flight and crashed into the ocean, killing all sixty-nine passengers aboard.

Bitter or better, what kind of person are our circumstances turning us into? Remember, it's all in how we view our circumstances. Do we truly look for the hand of God in their midst? King Saul viewed Goliath as a giant too big to fight. David, on the other hand, viewed Goliath as a giant too big to miss. Obstacle or opportunity, how are we truly viewing our circumstances?

"All I have seen teaches me to trust God for all I have not seen." —*Ralph Waldo Emerson*

Ralph Waldo Emerson, whose original profession and calling was as a Unitarian minister, left the ministry to pursue a career in writing and public speaking. He became one of America's best known and best loved 19th-century figures.

Has adversity left you bitter because you failed to see the

hand of God? Do you now desire the ability to see His hand at work in both the best and the worst of your present and future circumstances? If so, please pray the following:

> Dear heavenly Father, forgive me. Forgive me, because like Peter in the midst of my storms, I too have placed my eyes on the storm instead of the God of the storm. And having taken my eyes off my Savior, I find myself sinking down into my sea of bitterness. As my Lord rescued Peter, I am asking You to rescue me. Help me to see Your sovereign hand in all my present and future circumstances. Help me to understand there is absolutely nothing in my life that is beyond Your sovereign control. Work Your perfect work within my heart and life according to Your predestined plan for me, and in all things help me to trust You. I ask these things in Jesus' name. Amen.

5

A Young Lady, a Pastor, and a Dance Floor

A young lady asked her pastor if he thought it was wrong for her to hang out with her friends on weekends at a local nightspot, especially since all she was really doing, she said, was dancing.

Her pastor asked, "Do they serve alcohol there, and do some of the guys and ladies drink a little too much while they're there?

The young lady replied. "Yes, they serve alcohol there; and yes, some tend to drink too much while there, but not me. I don't drink."

Her pastor answered, "I would say it would be wrong for you as a Christian to hang out at that place."

"Why?" the young lady inquired.

The pastor smiled. "Because if you didn't already think it was wrong, you wouldn't be standing here asking me that question."

"Well, that's certainly not a good enough reason for me," she said angrily.

"As a rule, young lady," the pastor continued, "you should never hang out at any place you can't take Jesus along with you."

"Well, I take Jesus everywhere I go—even dancing," she retorted, noticeably irritated as she walked away.

That following weekend at the same local nightspot, the young lady was approached and asked to dance by a young man whom she had never met. As the two danced, the young man began whispering some very inappropriate things in the ear of the young lady.

She immediately became insulted. "I'll have you know, I am not that kind of a girl! I'm a Christian!"

Surprised, the young man immediately stopped dancing, looked straight at her, and inquired, "Then what are you doing in a place like this?"

Just like this story, many believers today argue over issues regarding our liberty as Christians. Although well-intentioned, some assemblies of believers have mistakenly imposed rules for conduct and activities based on what they believe to be scriptural mandates. Such actions lead to problems because a laundry list of do's and don'ts is not specifically spelled out for believers in the New Testament scriptures.

Regarding the matter of Christian liberty, we should always exercise caution when advising others in this area. Why? Because we could easily lead others into believing that a legal righteousness is acceptable to God. That, of course, would be very unfortunate in light of the Prophet Isaiah's inspired words (Isaiah 64:6).

> *But we are all as an unclean thing, and all our righteousnesses are as filthy rags; and we all do fade as a leaf; and our iniquities, like the wind, have taken us away.*

Furthermore, well-informed believers of the New Testament scriptures will absolutely not allow anyone, no matter how well-intentioned they are, to impose upon them a works religion.

Paul wrote in his first letter to the Corinthian believers,

All things are lawful unto me, but all things are not expedient; all things are lawful for me, but I will not be brought under the power of any. All things are lawful for me, but all things are not expedient; all things are lawful for me, but all things edify not (1 Corinthians 6:12; 10:23).

As believers in the exercise of our Christian liberty, Paul warns against activities that could lead us into bondage to anyone or anything other than Jesus Christ. Paul wanted believers to understand that some activities absolutely do not promote spiritual growth and intimacy with our Lord. Therefore, such activities are neither expedient, practical, or edifying to us. Paul taught that we as believers need to exercise our liberty responsibly; otherwise, we could unknowingly injure weaker Christians.

But take heed lest by any means this liberty of yours becomes a stumblingblock to them that are weak (1 Corinthians 8:9).

We can always argue that no matter what we do, there is absolutely no condemnation for anyone truly saved and cleansed by the blood of Jesus Christ (Romans 8:1). But for us to take such a hardline position, when our activities are causing other believers to stumble, simply reveals our failure to truly understand the real issue. There is a higher law at work here, which is the law of love. The real question isn't whether we have the *right* to do a particular activity. The real question is do we have enough of Christ's *love* in us to refrain from doing a particular activity, especially if we know it will mar our Christian witness and cause another Christian to falter and stumble.

Consider the following hypothetical example (I say hypothetical because neither of the authors of this book drink alcohol): Let's say I have a neighbor who has been an alcoholic for a number of years. God graciously gives me the opportunity to share my faith with him; and when I do, God brings my neighbor into a saving knowledge of Jesus Christ. As a result of my neighbor's recent conversion, he now looks up to me as being a mature Christian and places a great deal of confidence in me because of the way God used me to personally share with him the gospel message.

As a result of his conversion, he has now found the power in his life to abstain from the alcohol, which previously held him in bondage for many years. Then suppose one evening as I sit at the dinner table with my wife, enjoying a glass of wine (again hypothetically), the doorbell rings. Answering the door, I discover it is my neighbor—armed with Bible in hand. l invite him into my home, and he tells me he stopped by to ask me a couple of Bible questions.

During the course of our greeting as he enters our home, my neighbor suddenly spots the hypothetical bottle of wine and half-filled glasses on the table. He suspiciously questions me about the rights and wrongs of this. Then suppose I immediately direct his attention to the scriptures, showing him the glorious liberty we believers have in Jesus Christ and successfully convince him it is okay for my wife and me to drink alcoholic beverages. For my neighbor, this is just too good to

A Young Lady, a Pastor, and a Dance Floor

be true. Is there any wonder why he quickly embraces this doctrine regarding his liberty and asks me to pour him a tall drink as well?

Now, I find myself hypothetically faced with a major dilemma: After all, I am very aware of my neighbor's past bouts with alcoholism, but in light of what I just shared with him in the scriptures, how can I refuse his request? Wasn't it me who convinced him of the glorious liberty he now has as a believer? Paul wrote,

> But when ye sin so against the brethren, and wound their weak conscience, ye sin against Christ (1 Corinthians 8:12).

In the hypothetical example above, I convinced a fellow believer, who had been freed from his bondage to alcoholism, that in Christ he has the freedom to start drinking alcoholic beverages again. In doing so, you could say I may very well have destroyed his life (1 Corinthians 8:11). Paul's point is clear—if Jesus Christ loves my neighbor enough to have died for him, then as a follower of Jesus Christ, surely I should love my neighbor enough to refrain from any activity which could lead to my neighbor's demise. Paul exhorted,

> We then that are strong ought to bear the infirmities of the weak, and not please ourselves. Let every one of us please his neighbor for his good to edification (Romans 15:1-2).

Eugene H. Peterson's *The Message* renders this passage of scripture in the following way in contemporary language:

> Those of us who are strong and able in the faith need to step in and lend a hand to those who falter, and not just do what is most convenient for us. Strength is for service, not status. Each one of us needs to look after the good of the

people around us, asking ourselves, "How can I help?" (Romans 15:1-2 MSG).

Exercising our liberty responsibly as Christians means we realize in the choosing of our activities, it is not a matter of what pleases us, but rather what is best for our neighbor. The late pastor and evangelist J. Vernon McGhee put it this way: "You can swing your fist anywhere you please, but where my nose begins is where your liberty ends!"

Debating over questionable activities with other believers in the context of sin is both futile and fruitless. Such activities are not necessarily a matter of sin but rather of expedience. The questions we need to ask ourselves as believers regarding our activities and our conduct are:

- Is the activity I am doing right?
- Will the activity help me to grow in the knowledge and grace of Jesus Christ? (2 Peter 3:18)
- Will the activity damage or destroy my Christian witness such that God will not be glorified in my life? (Matthew 5:16)
- Will this activity lead me into bondage? (1 Corinthians 6:12)
- Will this activity cause other Christians to stumble? (1 Corinthians 10:23)

What about each of us? Have we asked ourselves these questions regarding our activities? Are our activities and conduct truly bringing glory to God? (1 Corinthians 10:31) Remember, true liberty in Jesus Christ is not the freedom to do a thing. True liberty in Jesus Christ is the freedom to *not* do a thing.

A Young Lady, a Pastor, and a Dance Floor

"The true follower of Christ will not ask, 'If I embrace this truth, what will it cost me?' Rather he will say, 'This is truth. God help me to walk in it, let come what may!'" —*Aiden Wilson (A.W.) Tozer*

A.W. Tozer was an American Protestant pastor and preacher, author, Bible conference speaker, and magazine editor.

Perhaps your activities have caused confusion and left others questioning the genuineness of your faith. If that is the case, and you desire God's power in your life to live as He has called you to live (Ephesians 4:1), then pray the following:

Dear heavenly Father, in Mark 8:34 Jesus is recorded as having said that if I would come after Him, I should deny myself, take up my cross, and follow Him. I recognize I do have liberty as a Christian. But I recognize something else as well, and that is I have not always exercised my liberty responsibly. I confess to You that in the past, I have not been willing to restrain my liberty or curtail my conduct out of my love for others. For that, I am truly sorry and ask Your forgiveness. From this moment forward, help me to understand how my activities as a Christian are either edifying or causing others to stumble. Convict my heart of those things in my life that are displeasing to You; and from this day forward, help my actions be motivated by a deep sense of love for You and others. I ask these things in Jesus' name. Amen.

6

A Professor, a Student, and a Bible

An agnostic professor's greatest delight was ridiculing Christians in his classes. One morning he asked his class of new students, "Is there anyone present among you who considers him or herself a Christian? Come on now, don't be bashful! If so, please raise your hand up high so I can see it."

One young fellow looked around at some of his classmates he knew were Christians but had chosen not to raise their hands. All alone, the boy slowly raised his hand up high as requested.

"Aw, I see we have one," acknowledged the professor. "Would you be so kind as to come down front and stand here beside me. Come on now. Don't be bashful."

The boy stood and walked to the front of the classroom. He stopped and turned to face his classmates as he stood beside the professor.

Almost immediately the professor mocked, "Young man, I think it very brave of you to do what you just did, but I believe your courage and faith may be somewhat misplaced and could be better spent on something else. For instance, I think it is totally absurd to believe in a God one cannot see! I have personally read the Bible myself throughout, and it does not make one bit of sense to me! I can't understand any of it!"

The boy turned and looked up at the professor and said,

"Sir, the Bible is a love letter from God to His children. That's what happens when you read someone else's mail." After saying this, the boy walked back to his desk and took his seat.

Paul wrote to the believers at the church in Corinth…
But we speak the wisdom of God in a mystery, even the hidden wisdom, which God ordained before the world unto our glory; which none of the princes of this world knew; for had they known it, they would not have crucified the Lord of glory. But as it is written, eye hath not seen, nor ear heard, neither have entered into the heart of man the things which God hath prepared for them that love Him. But God hath revealed them unto us by His Spirit: for the Spirit searcheth all things, yea, the deep things of God. For what man knoweth the things of a man, save the spirit of man, which is in him? Even so the things of God knoweth no man, but the Spirit of God. Now we have received, not the spirit of the world, but the Spirit, which is of God; that we might know the things that are freely given to us of God. Which things also we speak; not in the words which man's wisdom teacheth, but which the Holy Ghost teacheth; comparing spiritual things with spiritual. But the natural man receiveth not the things of the Spirit of God, for they are foolishness unto him; neither can he know them, because they are spiritually discerned (1 Corinthians 2:6-14).

Like this professor, nonbelievers reading the scriptures are unable to glean from its pages and mine from its depths the eternal treasures revealed in God's Word. Nonbelievers neither welcome divine wisdom nor understand it. It is a mystery to them because their minds have been veiled, blinded to divine truth (2 Corinthians 4:4). Having not been indwelled by the Holy Spirit, such individuals cannot possibly see the need to seek God's wisdom in their daily life. Therefore the very thought of God's abiding presence in every aspect of their life is to them foreign and pure nonsense (1 Corinthians 2:14). Unfortunately, what these individuals fail to realize is that a head full of knowledge without God leads to a life full of emptiness.

Quoting from the words of the Prophet Isaiah (Isaiah 64:4) Paul tells the believers in Corinth that no nonbeliever has ever seen, or heard, or understood in his or her heart, God's hidden wisdom, which is only revealed to those who truly love Him. There is no experience one may have or academic achievement one may accomplish that will make him or her a recipient of God's wisdom. Such wisdom comes only by divine revelation and is only possible for individuals who have the indwelling presence of the Holy Spirit within their lives. Likewise, to have the indwelling presence of the Holy Spirit within one's life is only possible for those who have opened the door to their heart and invited Jesus Christ to come into their lives (Revelation 3:20).

In order to become God's pupil, an individual must first become God's child. Jesus said no one comes to Him, the Son of God, unless first drawn by the heavenly Father. Jesus went on to say that God not only draws an individual but also teaches that individual His eternal truths (John 6:44-45). On the Gaza highway, Philip asked an Ethiopian eunuch, who was reading from a passage in the book of Isaiah, if he understood what he was reading (Acts 8:26-40). The eunuch responded with a question of his own: "How can I unless someone explains it to me?"

Philip then took the very same passage of scripture and showed the eunuch how it revealed God's redemptive plan for mankind in Jesus Christ. The eunuch immediately believed on Jesus Christ as Savior and was subsequently baptized by Philip. Before this Ethiopian eunuch could become a pupil of scripture and effectively communicate the salvation message to his own people, he had to first come to a saving knowledge of Jesus Christ.

Paul did not just stop at saying no nonbeliever has ever seen, or heard, or understood in his or her heart God's hidden wisdom. He also pointed out the fact that the Holy Spirit has enabled believers to see, hear, and understand with their hearts the wisdom, the truths, the insights, and the deep things of God (1 Corinthians 2:10). Indeed, as the student in the story correctly informed the professor, the Bible was not written for nonbelievers. Rather, it was written for us who believe; and as believers, we are to take its liberating message to nonbelievers.

What about us? Are we presenting the gospel to nonbelievers? Is our presentation effective? Do we have a burden for the souls of men and women, boys and girls? If so, we should consider the following: First, we *should not be argumentative* but be kind to everyone (2 Timothy 2:24-26). Secondly, we *should not become discouraged* if the individual we are sharing the gospel with does not come to faith in Jesus Christ during our presentation. Remember, God did not call us to be successful; He called us to be faithful. Thirdly, we should *remain prayerful* throughout our presentation that

God will deliver the individual from his/her sin bondage and bring them to a saving knowledge of Jesus Christ. Their eternity depends on it.

> "The scriptures are given not to increase our knowledge, but to change our lives." —*Dwight L. Moody*

Dwight L. Moody was an American evangelist and publisher of the 1800s. He founded the Moody Church, the Northfield School and Mount Hermon School in Massachusetts, the Moody Bible Institute, and Moody Publishers.

If you desire to have more boldness and become more effective in your presentation of the gospel to nonbelievers, please pray the following prayer:

> Dear heavenly Father, I realize that Your Word says in 1 Corinthians 1:18 that the preaching of the cross to them which are perishing is foolishness, but unto us who are saved it is the power of God. Give me, dear God, a genuine love and burden for the lost to see them saved. Your Word reveals Your heart on this matter. Your Word says in Acts 17:30 that You would have all men to come to repentance. Your Word says in 1 Timothy 2:4 that You would have all men to be saved and come to the knowledge of the truth. Your Word says in 2 Peter 3:9 that You are not willing that any should perish but that all should come to repentance. And, Your Word says in 2 Corinthians 5:20 that as a believer I have been called to be Your ambassador. As your ambassador, help me to remember the

words of my Savior who declared He came into this world to seek and to save those which are lost. Touch my heart and life so that from this day forward, I will be excited about being a part of my Lord's search and rescue team for lost humanity. I truly need Your help in sharing Your love letter with the nonbelievers around me. I pray this in Jesus' name. Amen.

7

Seeing God

An atheist, whose nine-year-old daughter had questions about God, sought to teach her his worldview and philosophy on life. The little girl had been talking to other children at school, and later that evening she approached her father, who was sitting comfortably on the sofa reading a book.

She joined her father on the sofa and asked him, "Daddy, can you tell me where God is?"

Her father looked at his daughter and responded with a simple smile. Then he placed the book he was reading aside momentarily, pulled out a pen and a piece of paper. He picked up his daughter and gently placed her on his lap. The father thought to himself that this would be a perfect opportunity to teach his daughter his disbelief in the existence of God. He laid the sheet of paper upon his book and wrote the words "God is nowhere."

He then invited his daughter to read aloud the answer to her question he had just written. The little girl stared momentarily at the sentence on the paper in front of her and then read, "God is now here."

Seeing God

Like the little girl in this story, it is possible for us to see God everywhere when we look for Him in everything. In the Sermon on the Mount Jesus declared, "Blessed are the pure in heart for they shall see God" (Matthew 5:8). Jesus was teaching that individuals, seeking to honor God in their hearts and lives, will not only be blessed with the spiritual vision to see God in the realm of time but will dwell in His presence throughout eternity as well. Jesus' words clearly reveal that the existence of God is not the issue. The real issue is an individual's ability to actually see and discern His presence. A person whose heart and eyes are perpetually fixed on things other than God lacks the ability to see God. When a person's eyes are on:

- **Things:** This leads to materialism, which impedes our ability to see God.
- **Circumstances:** This leads to our happiness or unhappiness, depending on outward conditions that we consider pleasing or displeasing. A focus on circumstances impedes our ability to see God.
- **Self:** This leads to pride, and pride impedes our ability to see God.
- **People:** This leads to idolatry, which impedes our ability to see God.

If you and I fail to see God, it is not because God is hiding from us. In fact, the Bible teaches God has chosen to reveal Himself to mankind through:

- **Creation** (Romans 1:20)
- **Man's conscience** (Romans 2:14-16)

- **Scriptures** (Romans 3:1-2)
- **His Son** (John 1:14; 14:9-11)

The reason nonbelievers cannot see God is because they are spiritually blind—a spiritual state in which Satan desires to keep them. Satan exercises power over nonbelievers through deception as he continually entices them to remain content in a spiritual matrix where they are convinced they are truly living life as it was meant to be lived. However, in reality, nothing could be further from the truth. In his last letter to the Corinthian church, Paul wrote the following regarding nonbelievers:

In whom the god of this world hath blinded the minds of them which believe not, lest the light of the glorious gospel of Christ, Who is the image of God, should shine unto them (2 Corinthians 4:4).

Even after Jesus physically healed a blind man (John 9:1-7), He later intercepted that same man in a crowd and asked him, "Dost thou believe on the Son of God?" (John 9:35) Jesus asked the question because He knew that although this man could now see physically, he was still blind spiritually. The greatest healing this man could possibly receive from Jesus was not in receiving his physical sight but rather in receiving his spiritual sight (John 9:36-38).

Unfortunately for many of us, we see only 1) what we have been taught to see and look for; and 2) what we choose to see. Some of us have been taught to look for the good in everything. Others of us have been taught to see only the bad. Some of us have an optimistic disposition while others have a pessimistic one. A glass partially filled with fluid is viewed by some as being half full and by others as half empty.

Seeing God

Of course, it really depends on whether the glass is being filled or emptied of fluid at the time.

Whether we are able presently to see God all about us or not, one day each of us will stand before Him in judgment (Hebrews 9:27). If we are believers, we will stand in judgment before God at the Bema Seat (1 Corinthians 3:11-15). If we are nonbelievers, we will stand in judgment before God at the Great White Throne judgment (Revelation 20:11-15). In short, eventually all mankind will see God in some type of judgment.

At times just as Peter did, we too find ourselves guilty of taking our eyes off our Lord (Matthew 14:22-31). When this happens for the Christian, we become overwhelmed by our circumstances.

"It is safe to tell the pure in heart that they shall see God, for only the pure in heart want to." —*C.S. Lewis*

C.S. Lewis was an Irish author and scholar. Lewis is known for his work on medieval literature, Christian apologetics, literary criticism, and fiction. He is best known for his children's series *The Chronicles of Narnia.*

If you are a Christian who is struggling presently to see the hand of God in your circumstances, please pray the following:

Dear heavenly Father, please forgive me. Forgive me because just as the Prophet Elijah did when being pursued by Jezebel (1 Kings 19) in the midst of harsh circumstances, I too find myself discouraged each time I've taken my eyes off You. Elijah looked for You in the great wind, but You were not in the wind. He looked for You in the mighty earthquake, but You were not in the earthquake. He looked for You in the fire, but You were not in the fire either. You came to Him in a still small voice, which spoke to Elijah's heart, and that same still small voice is speaking to my heart as well. Give me, O Lord, a heart that believes beyond all human logic, ears that hear beyond the audible, and eyes that see beyond the visible. Help me from this day forward to have the spiritual eyes to see You everywhere and know that I am never alone because You are ever present. I ask this in Jesus' name. Amen.

8

A Young Lady Witnessing in the Park

A young lady, with Bible in hand, was witnessing and sharing her faith with those passing by in the city park one day. A man, who had been observing her activities, approached her. He told her he considered himself an agnostic and wanted to show her how misguided and hopeless her faith really was.

The young lady quoted John 3:16 to him and said, "Well, sir, I believe the Bible is God's inspired word, and I believe what it says."

"That's nonsense," he argued. "The Bible is nothing but a collection of fables and unsubstantiated events that only an idiot would believe."

"But sir," the young lady said, "I believe the Bible is God's inspired word, and I believe what it says." She then quoted John 3:16 to him again.

The man became infuriated and attempted to intimidate the young lady by refuting everything she said to those passing by. However, the more he sought to intimidate and ridicule her faith, the more determined the young lady became.

Before long the man said, "Okay, tell me, can you point out any particular story in the Bible that has been proven?"

The young lady looked at him, quoted John 3:16, and

said, "Sir, I believe the Bible is God's inspired Word, and I believe what it says."

"Is that your only answer?" He laughed aloud. "Okay then, I'll pick a story myself. Take the story of Jonah, for example. Do you really expect me, or anyone for that matter, to believe he survived in the belly of a whale for three days? That, my dear, is absolutely ludicrous!"

The young lady replied, "Sir, the Bible says God prepared a great fish to swallow up Jonah, and the fish later spat him out on the coast of Nineveh. That is what the Bible says, and I believe it."

"Then what did Jonah eat and drink for three days?" he quizzed.

"I don't know, sir" she answered. "The Bible doesn't say. I guess I'll just have to ask Jonah when I get to heaven."

"Ah ha!" the man jeered loudly. "But what if Jonah isn't in heaven when you get there?"

"Then you can ask him yourself," she replied.

The single most important purpose of the church in this world is to glorify God, which is why being an effective witness and ambassador for Jesus Christ is so crucial. As believers we are to be the good ground Jesus spoke of in His parable of the sower and the seed (Matthew 13:3-9). Being witnesses for Jesus Christ is more than knocking on doors, traveling on mission trips, passing out tracts to strangers, and cornering co-workers, classmates, and peers. Being a witness for Jesus Christ is not limited to what we do—it is what we are.

A Young Lady Witnessing in the Park

The most effective witness we have is our very lives. Even when we are unaware, others are watching us and taking mental notes. If they are concerned with what we do, then we have the wonderful opportunity to show them what a difference Jesus Christ can make in a life committed to Him. In that way God is glorified in our lives (Matthew 5:16).

One young Christian man handed a tract to an older coworker at the construction site where they both worked. The older man quickly handed the tract back to the young fellow and said, "Don't bother giving that thing to me, sonny boy, cause I can't read no ways. But tell ya what I'll do. I'll watch your tracks." It has been said repeatedly that our life is the only Bible some sinner may ever have an opportunity to read. When someone reads our life and follows our tracks, will these things point them to Jesus Christ?

The young lady in this story exercised patience and wisdom in dealing with the scoffer. She absolutely refused to debate with him. Instead, she chose to give him God's Word and express her faith in it. Contending with nonbelievers over the validity of scripture oftentimes may seem like an exercise in futility. Like a postman, our responsibility is to prayerfully deliver the message with our mouths and our lives. What people do with the gospel message we deliver is really between God and them.

The best we can do is the best we can do; once the message has been delivered, we continue to pray for those who received it with the hope that God will give the increase. Some who hear the gospel will repent and embrace the saving message of Jesus Christ and His work at Calvary. Others will outright reject the message and remain in their sins. Jesus said to the blind man in the presence of the Pharisees,

For judgment I am come into this world, that they which see not might see; and that they which see might be made blind. And some of the Pharisees which were with him heard these words, and said unto Him, are we blind also? Jesus said unto them, If ye were blind, ye should have no sin; but now ye say, we see; therefore, your sin remaineth (John 9:39-41).

Jesus' words reveal to us that some who are religious but lost may never come to a saving knowledge of Jesus Christ. You may ask if it is God's will that some people be eternally lost. Not according to scripture. The Bible teaches God has called all men everywhere to repent (Acts 17:30). Scripture tells us God would have all men to be saved and come to the knowledge of the truth (1 Timothy 2:4). It also teaches God is not willing that any should perish but that all should come to repentance (2 Peter 3:9).

So how do Jesus' words above reveal that some religious people may never become saved? In John 9:39-41 Jesus is saying that

- individuals who are spiritually blind but continually insist they already spiritually see will not come to the only One who can truly open their spiritually blinded eyes and heart.
- individuals who walk in spiritual darkness yet continually insist they are walking in the light of God will not come to the only One who is the Light of the World and able to shine His light into their spiritually dark hearts.
- individuals who are spiritually lost but continually insist they are saved will not come to the Savior and be cleansed of their sin dilemma. Therefore these individuals, al-

A Young Lady Witnessing in the Park

though religious, are spiritually lost and therefore remain in their sin.

The greatest challenge today for Christians is not getting people saved. The greatest challenge today is getting people to realize they are lost. Until people are willing to acknowledge their sin dilemma and lost spiritual state, they see no need for Jesus, the only true Savior (Acts 4:12-13).

Alcoholics do not obtain sobriety and stay sober until they first acknowledge they have a drinking problem. Drug addicts do not get clean and stay clean until they first acknowledge they have a drug problem. And, sinners do not get saved by the blood of Jesus Christ until they first acknowledge they have a sin problem. If they are unwilling to do this, they remain in their sin.

Once confronted with the saving message of Jesus Christ, some will embrace it while others will reject it. Still others will not only reject it but will ridicule those sharing the gospel message. Being ridiculed for sharing our faith is no reason to be deterred from being used by God to plant the seed of faith and to water a seed already planted by another of God's witnesses. Jesus forewarned,

If the world hate you, ye know that it hated Me before it hated you. If ye were of the world, the world would love his own: but because ye are not of the world, but I have chosen you out of the world, therefore the world hateth you. Remember the word that I said unto you, The servant is not greater than his lord. If they have persecuted Me, they will also persecute you; if they have kept My saying, they will keep yours also. But all these things will they do unto you for My name's sake, because they know not Him that sent Me (John 15:18-21).

The message of the cross is incomprehensible to the human intellect because its message defies human logic. We must understand that God did not call us to think logically, but theologically about our relationship with Him (1 Corinthians 1:18). We should not become discouraged if we are ridiculed for sharing the glorious gospel message of Jesus Christ, our wonderful Savior. We should not be deterred if we are not eloquent in our presentation of this eternal truth. We can begin by simply sharing our personal testimony with others of how we became a Christian. This we can do while we are studying to become more knowledgeable of His word.

Remember, the resurrection power of Jesus Christ shining through our life is the most powerful witness for Jesus Christ we have.

> "Some want to live within the sound of church or chapel bell; I want to run a rescue shop within a yard of hell." —*C.T. Studd*

C.T. Studd is remembered both as a cricketer and missionary. As a cricketer, he played for England in some of the most famous Ashes matches. As an English Protestant missionary, he was one of the "Cambridge Seven" who offered themselves to Hudson Taylor for missionary service at the China Inland Mission.

What about you? Are you taking advantage of the opportunities God is giving you to share your faith and personal testimony? Would you like to be more effective as a Christian witness? If this is true, tell Him so. Please pray the following:

A Young Lady Witnessing in the Park

Dear heavenly Father, please touch my heart that I will make personal devotion and Bible study a priority in my life. I desire to be the most effective witness for You that You have called and empowered me to be. Please create within me the desire to be diligent in pursuing intimacy with You through prayer and a study of Your Word. And, Lord, may people around me see the light of Jesus Christ shining through my life from this day forward. I ask these things in Jesus' name. Amen.

9

Excuses

Uncle Willie was the kind of a man who could never admit when he was wrong under any circumstances! No matter the situation, in Willie's mind he was always justified in his behavior, even if no one else agreed with him.

One day old Willie wandered upon the camp of some of his friends who had been fishing all day. The men had gotten hungry earlier, gathered rocks and built a fire, and cooked some of the fish they had caught in a black cast iron skillet. After eating they just left the skillet sitting on top of the dying embers. Therefore when Willie spotted the skillet and saw no smoke rising up from the ashes, he assumed the skillet had cooled down. Without saying a word to any of the men who were busying themselves with their tackle boxes, Willie just walked over, kneeled down, and picked up the skillet with his right hand in order to remove it from the ash pile. The expression on Willie's face and the way he quickly tossed the hot skillet back down onto the hot embers clearly gave evidence that Willie realized he had made a huge mistake.

Having witnessed the entire incident, the men turned to Willie and one amusingly commented, "Pretty hot, huh, Willie?"

To which old Willie replied, "Naw, not really! It just doesn't take me long to look at a good cast iron skillet!"

Excuses

Like old Willie, sometimes the most difficult thing any of us can do is face the truth about ourselves. When we choose to offer up excuses rather than acknowledge any wrongdoing on our part, we give evidence that we are neither ready nor willing to face the truth.

Perhaps the most important first step for any of us to take is to see ourselves as God sees us. This, of course, means we are ready to abandon our truth and accept God's truth about everything, including ourselves. In the final analysis, God's truth is the only truth that really matters.

However, when we are unwilling to take this step, we find ourselves relegated to a perpetual state of pursuing an inner peace that always seems somehow to elude us. Why? It could very well be because we spend our days endlessly serving the triune god of me, myself, and I. Such a life cannot become self-less because it is too selfish. Such a life cannot become Christ-centered because it is too self-centered.

We need to seek the mindset of our Lord in all matters and in every area of our lives. Proverbs 3:5 commands us to trust the Lord with all of our heart and to never lean on our own understanding. When we embrace any agenda other than God's for our personal lives, we can become victimized by our own heart that can deceive us as Jeremiah warned in Jeremiah 17:9. While it is true we cannot always trust our own heart, it is equally true that we can always trust the heart of God. Proverbs 3:6 says that in all of our ways we should acknowledge the Lord, and He will direct our paths.

To trust the Lord with all our heart and to acknowledge

Him in all our ways makes us extremely sensitive to the still small voice of God. It enables us to see ourselves as He sees us and to discern how other people perceive us. Here is something to think about: Do others perceive us as loving? How about forgiving? Do our lives reflect the characteristics of the fruit of the Holy Spirit? (See Galatians 5:22-23.)

When used as a verb, the word "excuse" means to pardon or to forgive someone. However, when used as a noun, the word refers to a statement made or a reason given that frees one from blame or duty. The question we have to ask ourselves is how are we using this word in our own lives? Are we using it as a verb, victoriously walking in the forgiveness and blessings of our great God and Savior? Or are we using it as a noun, refusing to reflect the glorious light of our Savior because our pride will not allow us to admit when we are wrong?

Are we not called and empowered to follow the glorious example of our Lord by forgiving others, pardoning their transgressions against us, and refusing to be prideful? Or are we just simply making excuses as to why we refuse to do so? There can be no true change without until there is first a true change within.

What about you? Have you been guilty of excusing your words and your behavior, which inwardly you know are not Christlike? Are you ready to acknowledge this before God and allow Him to make you into the person He created you to be? In order to receive God's help, we must first recognize that we need God's help.

We must be willing to see ourselves as God sees us. God loves us just the way we are, but He loves us too much to leave us the way we are. Please understand that no sinner gets

Excuses

saved against his or her will, and no Christian spiritually grows against his or her will.

> "I used to ask God to help me. Then I asked if I might help Him. I ended up by asking Him to do his work through me." —*James Hudson Taylor*
>
> James Hudson Taylor was an English missionary and founder of the China Inland Mission

In this life, you and I cannot ultimately decide what happens *to us*, but we can decide what happens *in us*. If you are already a Christian, it is never too late to start doing the right thing. You may be asking what that is. If that is your question, please pray the following:

> Dear heavenly Father, I understand that it is only because of Your mercies that we are not consumed. Your compassions fail not. They are new every morning. Great is Your faithfulness. Lord, I am truly sorry for my waywardness and allowing my will, not Yours, to become my chief priority. Because of it, I have continually excused my words, my thoughts, and my behavior. I am sorry. I no longer want to talk, think, or live in a way that is contrary to Your will for my life. I now desire for me that which You desire for me—that in my life You will be glorified. I am asking You for Your forgiveness. Please cleanse me from all my sin, dear Lord. It is Your will, and Your will alone that I seek, and the life of Christ which I choose to live. Give me this day a servant's spirit and a surrendered heart before You. And from this moment forward give

me the power to do justly, to love mercy, and to walk humbly before You. I ask these things in Jesus' name. Amen.

10

A Lady and Her Revenge

A story is sometimes told of a lady who was bitten by a rabid dog during an era before an acceptable vaccine was developed for rabies. At the time she was bitten, the woman had no idea the dog was mad. However before long, she realized something was seriously wrong, so she made her way to the town's only doctor. After speaking with the lady about her symptoms followed by a thorough examination, the doctor regretfully informed the woman of the bad news.

He told her within a week she would be insane, and within another week she would be dead. Amid much weeping and tears, the woman pondered her situation and then suddenly requested from the doctor a pen and a pad. The doctor supplied her with both, and the woman hurriedly began writing down name after name of people she obviously knew.

Peeping over her shoulders and noticing the names on the pad, the doctor commented, "I assume those are the names of people you intend to put in your will?"

"Absolutely not!" the woman retorted, looking up. "These are the names of people I intend to bite!"

Unfortunately, like the woman in this story some people only live to get even. A slave to their passions, their likes and dislikes, these individuals find it practically impossible to refrain from acts of retaliation. However, this should never be our plight as Christians. Jesus taught and commanded us to:

Love your enemies, bless them that curse you; do good to them that hate you; pray for them who despitefully use and persecute you (Matthew 5:44).

God, through His Son Jesus, has not only called us to life, but He has also empowered us with His life to live differently. Jesus knew that the most effective weapon we have against our enemies is God's Word and a Spirit-filled life. Jesus also knew that the most effective response to hatred and rejection is love. When we are tempted to think and behave contrary to the scriptures, we have an opportunity to trust in God's Word, and in the God of the Word. No matter the circumstance, God is able to empower us to flee and resist any temptation to act or react in ways that are contrary to His will as revealed in His Word.

It is not God's will for us as Christians to respond to our friends and family with love, while responding to our enemies with vindictiveness and hatred. To do so is to eliminate any opportunity we have to reflect the light of Christ and to share our faith with others. Jesus taught:

For if ye love them which love you, what thank have ye? For sinners also love those that love them (Luke 6:32).

In this passage, Jesus' words compel us to answer the following question: If we only love the loveable, then how are we any different from the unredeemed? In this dog-eat-dog world in which we live, the only response the bitten know is to bite. The perfectly natural response to hatred is hatred. Fighting fire with fire is the world's way, but it is not God's way for those redeemed by the blood of Jesus.

As believers we do not have the right to hate others because our rights were nailed to Calvary's cross. At the cross of Jesus Christ, we surrendered our rights and became willing slaves to our Lord (1 Corinthians 6:19-20). Simply put—when you and I became Christians, we renounced our rights to hate and seek revenge against others. We are God's property, and as such it is His responsibility, not ours, to right any wrongs done to us. Paul wrote:

> *Dearly beloved, avenge not yourselves, but rather give place unto wrath: for it is written, Vengeance is mine; I will repay, saith the Lord* (Romans 12:19).

Responding to hatred and rejection in any way other than love is to respond like a nonbeliever. Such behavior on our part misrepresents the God we serve. The world is drawn, if by nothing else, by Spirit-led curiosity to the resurrection power of Jesus Christ (Philippians 3:10 and 1 Peter 3:15) which they witness being lived out in our lives. This is the power to love in spite of hate, to care and show compassion in spite of rejection, to pray in spite of retaliation, and to be not overcome by evil but overcome evil with good (Romans 12:21). The indwelling Holy Spirit empowers us to be different and to make a difference in the lives of those around us.

Tit for tat revenge only creates a vicious cycle for those who engage in its folly. However, when you and I call upon the power of our Lord to enable us to refuse to retaliate and repay another's hostility with hostility, we demonstrate to the world that greater is He that is in us than he that is in the world (1 John 4:4). The Apostle John wrote,

> Hereby, know we that we dwell in Him, and He in us, because he hath given us of His Spirit.... And we have known and believed the love that God hath to us. God is love; and he that dwelleth in love dwelleth in God, and God in him (1 John 4:13-16).

A vengeful, retaliatory spirit has no place in our lives as believers. Paul warned:

> Be ye angry, and sin not. Let not the sun go down upon your wrath. Neither give place to the devil (Ephesians 4:26-27).

An old preacher once commented, "When God forgave our sins, He cast them into the deepest part of the ocean and posted a no-fishing sign." When Jacob died, his sons who were older than Joseph became fearful of their brother Joseph, who was a very powerful ruler in Egypt, second only to Pharaoh. They feared Joseph would use their father's death as an opportunity to avenge the great evil his older brothers had perpetrated against him. Because of their fear, Joseph's older brothers approached and bowed themselves before him pledging:

> Behold, we be thy servants. And Joseph said unto them, fear not, for am I in the place of God? (Genesis 50:18-19)

Joseph's compassionate response revealed that he had already sincerely forgiven them years earlier, and he was grieved that they had not understood that fact. His words also revealed his understanding that it was the sovereign hand of God that brought about his imprisonment and stay in Egypt, not the treachery of his older brothers.

The next time you and I find ourselves tempted to get even or pay someone back for their wrong, like Joseph we should ask ourselves, "Am I in the place of God?" Rather than behaving like the woman in the story who listed the names of people she intended to bite, we should instead pray for those people and ask God's blessings upon their lives. Furthermore, as God gives us opportunity, we need to do good by them instead of evil (Galatians 6:10). To the believers in Rome, Paul wrote:

Therefore, if thine enemy hunger, feed him; if he thirst, give him drink; for in so doing, thou shalt heap coals of fire on his head (Romans 12:19b-20).

What about us? Are our minds and hearts crippled today by a vengeful, retaliatory spirit? What are we doing about the wrongs done to us by others? Are we putting them behind us, or are we keeping a record? Are we making a list and checking it twice? If God did not withhold forgiveness from us, why would we withhold it from others who seek our forgiveness as we sought God's?

Perhaps we withhold forgiveness because we feel the individual does not deserve our forgiveness. In some instances, we are probably right—perhaps they don't! But here is the larger question: Did you and I deserve God's forgiveness?

When you and I refuse to forgive someone who seeks our forgiveness, we become his/her slave. Their presence and the very thought of them seizes our thinking, our emotions, and our actions, and hold us captive. If we are Christians, the good news is that God has liberated us from sin's power through the blood of Jesus Christ, and we are no longer slaves to sin (Romans 6:6).

"I can forgive, but I cannot forget, is only another way of saying, I will not forgive. Forgiveness ought to be like a canceled note—torn in two, and burned up, so that it never can be shown against one." —*Henry Ward Beecher*

Henry Ward Beecher was a prominent, theologically liberal American Congregationalist clergyman and social reformer, and famous speaker of the 1800s.

Be honest—if your thoughts, emotions, and actions have been enslaved by an unforgiving spirit, and you desire to be free, please pray the following:

Dear heavenly Father, please help me to walk and live in the freedom You purchased for me through the sacrifice of Your beloved Son Jesus Christ at Calvary. I confess to You I have a difficult time loving certain individuals. In my own strength, I find this an impossible task. But I know with You, all things are possible. Therefore, I am asking You to forgive me and help me to stop withholding forgiveness from those who seek it because You did not withhold forgiveness from me when I sought it. Help me to love everyone, including those who consider themselves my enemy. Your Word tells me in Matthew 6:15 that if I forgive not men their trespasses, neither will You forgive me of mine, and it is not my desire to be out of fellowship with You. Give me, I pray, a forgiving spirit and a surrendered heart from this day forward. I ask these things in Jesus' name. Amen.

11

One and Forty-Nine

In the absence of one student that particular day, forty-nine students were secretly asked by a professor to take part in an upcoming experiment. The professor drew and labeled two chalk lines as "A" and "B" on the board. In spite of the fact that it was obvious to all forty-nine students present that line "B" was at least four to five inches longer than line "A", as part of the experiment, the professor instructed the forty-nine students to all agree that the line labeled as "A" was the longer of the two lines. Once the students understood these simple instructions, they were asked not to share that information with anyone. Afterwards, they were dismissed and instructed to return at their designated class time on the next day.

The next day the students all reconvened in the classroom as scheduled. However, this time they were joined by the student who had been absent the day before and was unaware of the professor's experiment. The professor directed all the students' attention to the chalkboard and instructed them to raise their hands when he pointed to the longer of the two lines already drawn in chalk on the board. When the professor pointed to the shorter line labeled "A", all forty-nine of the students quickly raised their hand in agreement that this was the longer of the two lines.

One and Forty-Nine

The unsuspecting student slowly looked all around the classroom and was utterly baffled and amazed to see all hands up, except his, agreeing line "A" was the longer of the two lines. Unwilling to be different, the student slowly slipped his hand up in the air along with his classmates.

Most of us dismiss "peer pressuritis" as a disease which afflicts only the young. However, this malady is no respecter of age or persons—striking both young and old, Christian and non-Christian alike. For the Christian, succumbing to peer pressure is merely symptomatic of a more grave condition—misplaced priorities. When our priorities are wrong, the first thing that suffers is our relationship with God. And when our relationship with God suffers, the power and effectiveness of our Christian witness suffer as well.

Many of us would quickly argue, "Wait just a minute, I would never have raised my hand like that student did in the classroom surrounded by forty-nine other students." Well, let's look at this in a little different way. When we laugh aloud at those really crude, inappropriate jokes told by non-Christian coworkers, classmates, and friends, are we not raising our hand? When we intentionally ostracize someone because a friend, family member, or associate of ours dislikes that particular person, are we not raising our hand? When we engage in activities on our job or at school that we know violate Christian principles we claim to embrace just to be considered a team player, are we not raising our hand? When we overspend, trying desperately to keep up with the Joneses, are we not raising our hand?

It's been said, "Any old dead fish can flow downstream." It takes a live fish to swim upstream against the current. Likewise, it takes a Christian with the right priorities and convictions to march against the current tide of popular opinion and peer pressure. The psalmist declared,

Blessed is the man that walketh not in the counsel of the ungodly; nor standeth in the way of sinners, nor sitteth in the seat of the scournful. But his delight is in the law of the Lord, and in His law doth he meditate day and night (Psalm 1:1-2).

Our unsaved friends and associates can have a profound effect on our lives. However, the psalmist wisely points out God's blessings are promised to believers who are not distracted by such associations. Instead, the blessed believer delights in studying and meditating upon the scriptures to glean from them daily wisdom and insight for living. The psalmist goes on to say,

And he shall be like a tree planted by the rivers of water that bringeth forth his fruit in his season; his leaf also shall not wither and whatsoever he doeth shall prosper (Psalm 1:3).

Nowhere in scripture are we commanded to avoid associations with nonbelievers. There is no better way to witness to someone than through association. However, believers cannot afford to become distracted and influenced by such associations. To prevent this from happening, we are encouraged to continually read and internalize God's Word.

The blessing promised when we faithfully do such is that others will see in our lives the characteristics of spiritual fruit (Galatians 5:22-23) because God has taken His rightful position of being first in our hearts and our lives (Matthew 6:33).

"Character is always lost when a high ideal is sacrificed on the altar of conformity and popularity."
—*Charles Spurgeon*

Charles Spurgeon was a British Reformed Baptist pastor who still remains highly influential among Reformed Christians of different denominations.

What about you? Have you succumbed to peer pressure? Are your associations with nonbelievers overly influencing you? Do you want—do you need—God's help in getting your priorities straight? If this is true, tell Him so. Please pray the following:

> Dear heavenly Father, I admit I have not been seeking first Your kingdom and Your righteousness as Jesus commanded us to do. I have allowed myself to become distracted by my associations and the lures of this world, and I am so very sorry. Please forgive me and cleanse me. Touch my heart right now and please be first in my heart and life. Give me wisdom and power for each day to obey You and to walk before You with an upright heart. I ask these things in Jesus' name. Amen.

12

Reasoning with the Unreasonable

A medical student, serving part of his internship in a mental institution, encountered a patient who continually walked the corridors of the hospital, declaring to everyone he was dead. Neither the staff nor the patients ever paid any attention when he insisted to them he was deceased. They simply just overlooked him—everyone, that is, except this new intern, who made it his business to find out everything he could about this particular patient who was clearly disturbed. Irritated by the patient's daily insistence that he was dead, this intern took it upon himself to straighten the man out so he would stop this nonsense of claiming he was dead. One morning the intern stopped the disturbed man in the hallway, sat him down, and politely informed the patient he was alive and certainly not dead.

"Oh yes, I'm dead all right. No pulse, no heartbeat, nothing! Yes sir, indeed, I'm dead!" the man adamantly insisted. "I've been dead for a very long time."

"You're not dead," the new intern repeated, determined to make his point. "Just look at yourself. You can see, smell, touch, breath, and even sit upright in that chair. You're as alive as anyone in this place."

"No, no, you're wrong! I'm dead all right. No pulse, no heartbeat, nothing! Been dead a long time."

Reasoning with the Unreasonable

The debate between the two went on for a few more minutes, and the intern became noticeably frustrated due to his inability to get the patient to listen to reason. This amused a couple of the staffers who sat nearby observing the discussion.

In a final attempt to reason with the disturbed man, the intern asked, "Tell me, do dead people bleed?"

"How silly," the man replied. "Everyone knows dead people don't bleed."

"But people who are alive do bleed—correct?" coached the intern, hoping for agreement.

"Correct," the man said, agreeing.

To the surprise of the observing staffers, the intern quickly pulled a pocketknife from his pocket, opened it, and grabbed the patient's hand. Using the pointed end of the blade, he quickly pricked the tip of the patient's index finger. Immediately the man's finger began bleeding. As it did, the man sat silently in awe and utter bewilderment, watching the blood drip from his finger down onto the floor below.

Confident he had proven his point, the intern turned his attention to the other staffers and smiled before turning back to the patient sitting before him. "Well, what do have to say now?"

The man, in absolute amazement, slowly looked up into the face of the intern and remarked, "Hey, how about that? Dead people do bleed!"

As strange as it may seem, even sound reasoning sometimes proves futile when talking to some individuals. Good old common sense may be at the very top of the menu, but there are those times when no one seems to be ordering any. When Paul was leaving Ephesus for Macedonia, he urged Timothy to stay behind in Ephesus in order that he might seek to put an end to the false doctrine being promulgated by false teachers (1 Timothy 1:1-5). Paul knew that what he was asking of Timothy would be no easy task, so he encouraged and reminded Timothy to stir up the gift of God within him that he received earlier when Paul had prayed and blessed him.

However, most of us have already learned that when we are attempting to persuade others whose minds are already steadfastly set on their own agenda, even employing scriptural truths to convince them otherwise does not preclude it from becoming a very daunting task.

It is like those times when a father sits down with his fifteen-year-old son and attempts to explain to him why he cannot borrow the family car on Saturday night, the day after receiving his learner's permit. It is like those times when a mother tries to console and convince her thirteen-year-old daughter that her feelings for Johnny, who just broke up with her, are not true love but simple infatuation. Many of these discussions end the way they begin—a failure to successfully reason with the unreasonable.

Sharing our faith with some nonbelievers at times can be a very challenging experience even for Christians who are well prepared. Regarding the spiritual unreasonableness of nonbelievers, Paul in his letter to the Corinthian church wrote:

> *But the natural man receiveth not the things of the Spirit of God; for they are foolishness unto him; neither can he*

know them, because they are spiritually discerned (1 Corinthians 2:14).

Nonbelievers lack the supernatural life that comes only by the indwelling presence of the Holy Spirit in those who have truly trusted Jesus Christ as Savior. Without this abiding inner presence of God, it is impossible for these individuals to discern spiritual truths. However, the indwelling Spirit of God for us Christians illuminates, reveals, and opens up our understanding of the things of God.

I personally am familiar with a similar situation to that of the intern in the story. Another individual, whom I will call Josh, told me of a conversation he'd had with a mutual acquaintance of ours named Luke.

According to Josh, when he sat down and attempted to speak to Luke about spiritual matters, it was like speaking with someone from another planet. He asked me if I would make an appointment with Luke and attempt to share the gospel message with him. I agreed to do so and within a few days, Luke agreed to meet with me at my home. It was a nice warm summer day when Luke arrived at my house, so we took two chairs and sat comfortably in my front yard under the cool shade of two large maple trees. After exchanging greetings and a few pleasantries, Luke let me know immediately he was already "right with God."

According to Luke, his parents had forced him to attend church when he was a child, but when he became a teenager, he stopped attending and never went back.

During the course of our discussion, he made several statements like, "Most preachers can't hold a light to my knowledge of the Bible. Why, most of 'em eat pork and everyone knows that's a sin!"

I deliberately avoiding debating Luke over what he knew and did not know of the scriptures. I was more interested in attempting to get him to share with me what he considered to be his personal encounter with the Savior. But, throughout the entire conversation, Luke continued to ignore any attempts on my part to get him to share such an event in his life. It also became evident Luke believed a good offense would be his best defense against any Spirit-led assessment of his standing with God. So throughout our time together, he continued to attack all ministers and laymen and questioned their genuineness as believers. I asked him if he had taken the opportunity to visit any churches, given that it had been years since he attended one. He reminded me again that he did not attend any churches because he knew more about the Bible than most preachers. He also remarked that most preachers were not eloquent enough in their presentations for someone like him. He made a point to tell me that he reads the dictionary as a hobby. In addition to knowing a lot of what he referred to as "big words" from the dictionary, he also informed me that he was fluent in Latin as well.

Redirecting the conversation, I asked how his friends and acquaintances who knew him best perceived him. He asked me what I meant by that question, so I quickly rephrased my question.

"You told me earlier you were right with God. Tell me, do those who know you best consider you to be a Christian?"

"I really don't care what other people think of me. Whether they think I'm a Christian or non-Christian doesn't really matter," he answered sarcastically.

I decided to push a little further in this area. "Tom and John are good friends of yours. You guys hang out together all the time. Do Tom and John think of you as a Christian?"

"Why they wouldn't know a Christian if one jumped up and bit 'em," he laughed. "Tom and John think a Christian is someone who reads their Bible and goes around telling everybody about Jesus Christ."

Bible reading and witnessing certainly do not make one a Christian, but these are activities each of us as Christians should be doing, I thought to myself.

"In fact," he continued, "I've never met a real Christian in all my years of living in this state." Luke was approximately twenty-nine years old. By now the hair on the back of my neck was standing, and I certainly needed the help of the Holy Spirit to keep Luke from knowing he had just insulted me and a myriad of great Christian witnesses I knew in our community.

"Wait a minute, Luke," I said. "Doesn't the scripture declare that anyone who truly repents and places his or her faith in Jesus Christ and His substitutionary death and sacrifice at Calvary becomes a Christian? Are you saying individuals who have done this don't have eternal life?"

"Oh, no," Luke said. "I'm only saying that even though they're Christians, they're not real Christians as I see it." Then Luke reiterated how he had too much knowledge to waste his time sitting in some church, listening to men in pulpits who knew far less than he did.

Finally, I asked, "Luke, you said yourself you believe you have all this Bible knowledge and insight into the scriptures. The Bible teaches us that spiritual gifts are given to an individual for the profit of others within the body of believers. Don't you feel you should be in church sharing these special gifts of yours with others?"

"Oh no," he replied, standing to his feet. "My gift is to sit at home and read my dictionary and Bible to myself."

After saying this, he politely excused himself and left. As he did, I prayed for Luke and thought of the story of the disturbed man and the intern, and wondered to myself should I have asked him, "Do dead people bleed?"

> "You might as well try to hear without ears or breathe without lungs, as to try to live a Christian life without the Spirit of God in your heart." —*D.L. Moody*

D.L. Moody was an American evangelist and publisher of the 1800's. He founded the Moody Church, the Northfield School and Mount Hermon School in Massachusetts, the Moody Bible Institute, and Moody Publishers.

What about you today? Ever have any experiences like that when attempting to share your faith with a nonbeliever? It is incumbent upon each of us as believers to be prayerful and remain students of the scriptures for we never know when God is going to give us another opportunity to share our faith with a nonbeliever. We should pray continually that we will be the witnesses God has called and empowered us to be (Luke 18:1; Matthew 5:16).

We should also be studying the scriptures to constantly equip ourselves for service (2 Timothy 2:15; 1 Peter 3:15). In sharing our faith, we must stay sensitive to the leading of the Holy Spirit. And remember, God did not call us to be successful; He called us to be faithful. The best any of us can do is to be well prepared and to plant a gospel seed or water a gospel seed already planted by someone else. The increase is up to God (1 Corinthians 3:6).

Reasoning with the Unreasonable

If you would like to be more effective as a witness for Jesus Christ, please pray the following:

Dear heavenly Father, I know You have commissioned us as Your body of believers to go out into the world around us and take the gospel message. I also understand that everything we need in order to do that, You have already provided in Your written Word, through a saving knowledge of Jesus Christ, through the leading of the Holy Spirit, and through the various spiritual gifts You have given to members of the church. I desire to be an effective witness for You, and I want to be what Jesus referred to as good soil that the seeds fell among, multiplying themselves some thirty-, some sixty-, some a hundred-fold. In my own strength and wisdom, I cannot make this happen. However, in Your strength, all things are possible. Give me opportunities to share my faith and help me to stay prepared and ready for those opportunities. I ask this in Jesus' name. Amen.

13

The Bigger They Come, the Harder They Fall

A story is told about some wise counsel a mother whale imparted to her baby whale. She told her offspring, "Remember, when you get full of air and go to the top to blow, that's usually when you get harpooned!"

Being prideful is having a high opinion of one's own importance or superiority. If pride is in an individual's heart, eventually it will manifest itself in that individual's words and conduct. The Proverbs writer wrote,

Pride goeth before destruction, and a haughty spirit before a fall (Proverbs 16:18).

When an individual's nose is high in the air, stumbling over the little potholes in his or her path is inevitable. Having a false sense of one's own self-worth is borne out of one's overconfidence and self-deception. Eventually such an individual with this mindset, who fails to change his/her way of thinking, is headed for a fall (1 Corinthians 10:12).

James, the brother of our Lord, and Peter, the Apostle, echoed the words of the Psalmist in Psalm 138:6 when both

The Bigger They Come, the Harder They Fall

encouraged believers to pursue humility: "God...giveth grace unto the humble (James 4:6b; 1 Peter 5:5b)."

A prideful individual who lacks humility, on the other hand, is one who is self-centered, not Christ-centered and sits upon the throne of his/her own heart—the place reserved for God alone. That is why these very same scriptures (James 4:6a; 1 Peter 5:5a) teach that "God resisteth the proud."

When the Proverbs writer lists the seven things which God hates and is detestable to Him, an attitude of pride tops this list (Proverbs 6:16-19).

The Proverb writer goes on to declare,

Every one that is proud in heart is an abomination to the Lord; though hand join in hand, he shall not be unpunished (Proverbs 16:5).

Notice the warnings of the Proverbs writer to those who are prideful in Proverbs 16:5;18 and also in Proverbs 29:23. He warns the prideful their path ultimately leads to destruction and punishment, and their direction is downward. Even the Prophet Ezekiel, when listing the great sins of Sodom which God destroyed by fire and brimstone (Genesis 19), identified pride at the very top of their list of sins (Ezekiel 16:49).

James, Peter, the Psalmist, and the Proverbs writer, all declare that the recipients of God's grace are those who are humble and lowly. The only real antidote for pride is humility.

What exactly is humility? Before identifying what humility is, let's identify what it is not. Humility is not thinking lowly of oneself and highly of one's own lowliness. Instead, humility is the taking of our eyes off ourselves, as we run with patience this Christian race before us, and fixing our eyes instead upon Jesus, the Author and Finisher of our faith (Hebrews 12:1-2).

People say there is no set formula for serving God as believers because each person has to work out his or her own salvation with fear and trembling (Philippians 2:12). True, we do have to work out our own salvation. However, I believe there is a two-part formula I think we all should follow:

1. **A Perfect Heart:** We need to beg God daily to give us a heart that is perfect and upright before Him as we seek to walk obediently in accord with the scriptures. Second Chronicles 16:9 tells us God's eyes continually look throughout the earth for individuals whose hearts are perfect toward Him. We should beg God daily to turn our hearts toward Him that in our lives He may be glorified, His body of believers edified, and the spiritually lost evangelized.

2. **A Surrendered Life:** We need to beg God daily to give us a humble spirit and a surrendered life.

The king's heart is in the hand of the LORD, as the rivers of water: he turneth it whithersoever he will (Proverbs 21:1).

In this passage, we see the direction of a king's heart is subject to the Lord's will. If God turns kings' hearts in whichever direction He chooses, how much more ours when we desire for our hearts and lives to become totally surrendered to Him?

To ask God for a humble spirit is to come before Him not seeing our importance but our worthlessness apart from

Him; not seeing what we possess but what we lack; not depending on our knowledge but acknowledging our ignorance; not trusting in our strength but recognizing our weakness apart from Him; and not depending on ourselves, but totally upon Him.

In the book of Micah, a rhetorical question is asked regarding what it takes to please God (Micah 6:6-7). The prophet answers this question in verse 8:

> *He hath showed thee, O man, what is good; and what doeth the Lord require of thee; but to do justly, and to love mercy, and to walk humbly with thy God* (Micah 6:8).

"He that is down need fear no fall, He that is low no pride." —*John Bunyan*

John Bunyan was a preacher and a writer who was born at Harrowden, in the Parish of Elstow, England. Bunyan is best known for writing *The Pilgrim's Progress*, arguably the most famous Christian allegory ever published.

What about you? Has pride gotten in your way of serving and pleasing God? Remember, whatever God does not send up is subject to coming back down. If pride has interrupted your fellowship with and your service to God, and you desire for God to change your heart, tell Him so.

Please pray the following:

> Dear heavenly Father, I recognize that I have become prideful, and I stand without excuse before You. My Savior was humble, and as His follower, I realize it is impossible to serve You if I am prideful. Forgive me

for this sin and redirect my heart toward You and Your will for my life. From this day forward may my walk be characterized by a life of humility. I ask these things in Jesus' name. Amen.

14

Senior Citizens and a Joy Ride

In the late 1950s, a teenage boy and his girlfriend spent a great deal of time joy riding in his '57 Chevy. His girlfriend would sit so close to him in the car, he barely had enough room to steer the vehicle. Over the course of time, the two eventually married. They raised a family together and as the years rolled on, the two aged their way into senior citizens. Whenever this elderly couple traveled together, the wife would position herself comfortably on the other side of the car.

One evening while the two of them were out and about in their car, they pulled up and stopped at a red light. The old woman glanced over to her right just as another car pulled up and stopped right beside theirs. The older woman noticed it was a teenage couple sitting in the other vehicle. The teenage boy barely had enough room to steer the vehicle because his girlfriend was sitting so close to him.

Reminiscing, the old woman smiled and turned to her husband. "Honey," she said pointing at the other car, "look over there at that teenage couple. They are so adorable. Remember when we used to sit like that in the car?"

The elderly gentleman smiled, looked at his wife, and quietly replied, "I haven't moved!"

If the Shoe Fits

The second book of Samuel records an event in which the prophet Nathan informs King David of a very hideous act perpetrated in his kingdom against a poor man by his rich neighbor. What the prophet actually described to the king in the form of a parable was the evil deed David himself had committed against his own servant Uriah, the Hittite (2 Samuel 11-12). However, having become blinded by his own sin, David was unable to recognize himself as the villain in Nathan's parable. After hearing of the rich man's wicked actions, David became enraged and declared to Nathan that as surely as the Lord lives, whoever this rich man was, he would be put to death. Imagine the king's shock when Nathan revealed to David the identity of the rich man: "Thou art the man (2 Samuel 12:7)."

Perhaps if some of us as Christians discovered just how far away from an intimate relationship with God we have strayed, we too would be just as shocked as King David. Like the king, we have unwittingly allowed our relationship with our Lord to erode and become lukewarm. Perhaps this is inevitable when:

1. Our relationship with our Lord ceases to be the number one priority in our lives, and
2. Our allegiance to our Lord becomes divided due to an unchecked infatuation with the lures and enticements of this worldly system in the form of fortune, fame, power, and pleasure.

In his first epistle to the Corinthian believers, Paul

teaches that spiritually speaking, there are only two kinds of people—the saint and the sinner. In the same passage of scripture, Paul also teaches that there are only two kinds of saints—the carnally minded and the spiritually minded.

The carnally minded Christian caters to the appetites of his or her fleshly nature and therefore lives with unconfessed sin in his or her life. Unfortunately, carnally minded Christians are no stranger to spiritual defeat. The spiritually minded Christian, though blameless, is not sinless but continually seeks God's guidance (Proverbs 3:5-6) and God's cleansing (1 John 1:7-9) in every area of his or her life. Therefore, the spiritually minded Christian is no stranger to spiritual victory.

To be carnally minded means our relationship with Jesus Christ is, at best, lukewarm. To be spiritually minded means our relationship with Jesus Christ is our number one priority.

Have we allowed distance to come between the Lord and us? If so, remember that God has not moved.

James, the brother of our Lord, teaches how we may close the gap and eliminate the distance between God and us. James urges that we should...

- Humble ourselves before God (James 4:6).

- Stop resisting Christ's lordship over our lives and instead, surrender to it (James 4:7).

- Resist the temptations and snares of the devil who would have us to be self-reliant rather than God-reliant, self-centered as opposed to Christ-centered, and selfish as opposed to selfless (James 4:7).

- Draw nigh (come near) to God, knowing if we do, God will draw nigh to us (James 4:8).

- Cleanse our hands and purify our hearts. In short, address those things in our lives that place distance between the Lord and us (James 4:8).
- Grieve and truly mourn over our sin. In other words, repent. (James 4:9).

After being confronted with his own sin, King David repented and sought to eliminate the distance between God and him. Consider his words...

Have mercy upon me, O God, according to Thy lovingkindness; According unto the multitude of Thy tender mercies blot out my transgressions. Wash me thoroughly from mine iniquity and cleanse me from my sin. For I acknowledge my transgressions; and my sin is ever before me. Against Thee, Thee only, have I sinned, and done this evil in Thy sight; that Thou mightest be justified when Thou speakest, and be clear when Thou judgest. Create in me a clean heart; O God; and renew a right spirit within me. Restore unto me the joy of Thy salvation (Psalm 51:1-4; 10,12).

"No one who really wants to count for God can afford to play at Christianity." —Harry Allen (H.A.) Ironside.

H.A. Ironside was an American Bible teacher, pastor, and author.

If your relationship with God has eroded into lukewarmness, but you now desire the same closeness with God that He desires with you, tell Him. Remember, God is as close as the mention of His name. Please pray the following...

Dear heavenly Father, as David repented and prayed, I too repent and am asking for Your forgiveness. Forgive me for not seeking first Your kingdom and Your righteousness but allowing other things to have greater priority in my life than You and Your will for my life. Forgive me for my divided allegiance and my unchecked infatuation with the lures of this world. You said in Your Word in Revelation 3:15, You would have us to be hot or cold but not lukewarm. I desire to be spiritually hot, Lord, and I sincerely mean it. Help it to be so in my life from this day forward. I ask this in Jesus' name. Amen.

15

A Pardon from the King

A king decided to visit the prison house in his kingdom where a number of individuals were incarcerated. As he approached the first cell, the prisoner leaped to his feet and rushed forward toward the King, pleading, "O King, have mercy on me! I'm an innocent man!"

Reading from a scroll given to him by one of the guards, the king said to the man, "But, sir, it says here you are guilty of murder!"

"Lies, all lies," the man insisted.

"I see," the king responded before moving on to another cell, as another prisoner, spotting the king, jumped to his feet and raced forward pleading,

"Have mercy on me, O King, for I am an innocent man!"

Again, reading from the same scroll, the king looked at the man and said, "But, sir, it says here you were caught cheating your employer's customers and pocketing the money."

"Lies, O King, all lies! You have to believe me. I'm an innocent man."

"I see," the king responded before moving on to another cell, and another prisoner. The king visited cell after cell after cell and prisoner after prisoner after prisoner, and each begged for mercy, insisting they were innocent. But none re-

A Pardon from the King

ceived the king's pardon. Finally, the king visited a cell wherein sat a man who neither jumped to his feet when he saw the king nor entreated him for a pardon. The man sat teary eyed and broken.

"So, tell me, why are you here?" asked the king as though he did not already have the information on the scroll he carried in his hands.

"Because, O King, I deserve to be here. My family was hungry, and I stole from my neighbor's field to feed them. I should have asked my neighbor, but knowing the kind of man my neighbor was, I knew he wouldn't help us. So, I stole from him and got caught. My family's hunger is no excuse for what I did! So I'm here, O King, because I truly deserve to be."

Hearing the man's confession, the king turned and summoned his jailer to his side. "Quickly, set this man free at once. We cannot have this guilty man staying here in my prison among all these innocent people!"

Not all the prisoners in this story felt the same way about their predicament as the last prisoner the king spoke to and pardoned. In spite of that, all these prisoners, including the one pardoned, still had one thing in common—each was reaping the consequences of his own bad decisions.

This does not mean that suffering is limited to only those who make bad decisions. Suffering, sooner or later, finds each of our addresses. Believers do not have exempt status from suffering. It therefore behooves us as Christians to discover what types of suffering are unavoidable and what types are avoidable.

First, without going into an exhaustive list, let's examine a few reasons why people suffer. Let's start at the very beginning. The Garden of Eden in which God created man and woman was a perfect worry- and suffering-free environment (Genesis 1:26-2:25). When Adam and Eve chose to disobey God's command to not eat from the tree of the knowledge of good and evil (Genesis 2:16-17; 3:6; and 1 Timothy 2:13-14), they committed the original sin and were subsequently driven from the Garden of Eden (Genesis 3:22-24) to live in a fallen creation.

Unlike in the Garden of Eden, creation fell due to the first family's sin; and as a result of this original sin, suffering, sickness, and death entered into the world. When Adam and Eve committed the original sin, they suffered the loss of their innocence. And the loss of that innocence caused the two of them to immediately flee from the voice of God in the cool of the day and seek refuge from Him as though such a place could exist.

The sin nature is passed down through the seed of the man. In short, Adam, representing mankind's federal head, passed his sin nature on to all mankind through his seed. Mankind has been running from the voice of God every since. In fact, the fallen nature we inherited begins at life's earliest stage (Psalm 51:5).

While it true that all suffering is the result of sin—either original or personal sin, it can also be argued that not all suffering is a bad thing in the lives of God's people. Some suffering can serve as a useful catalyst to facilitate spiritual growth and maturity in our lives as believers. Let's look at a few reasons why

Individuals suffer:

1. Suffering can facilitate spiritual growth. God can use suffering to raise a believer's level of spirituality by rightly relating him or her to their circumstances. For example, we may pray for God to remove what we believe to be a problem in our life; and in response to our prayer, God may choose to remove it. Or God may choose to respond differently and not remove what we view as a problem. Why? It could be that God has chosen to use it in our lives to raise our level of spirituality. How does He raise our level of spirituality? By teaching us through our problem to depend and trust in Him no matter what we are experiencing. If we are honest with ourselves, we discover retrospectively the problem God chose to leave in our lives ultimately worked out for our good and to His glory (Romans 5:3-5).

2. Suffering can be the result of one taking a stand for Jesus Christ. Jesus preached, "Blessed are they which are persecuted for righteousness' sake." To suffer affliction or be persecuted emotionally or physically because we follow Jesus Christ is not something most would volunteer to do. However, Jesus encourages us through His words that all suffering for His sake is accompanied by God's blessings in our lives (Matthew 5:10-11 and Luke 6:22).

3. Suffering can be the result of one's failure or refusal to seek God's divine intervention. Our failure to pray and seek God's guidance in our circumstances can oftentimes lead to needless suffering in our lives. The Psalmist teaches us in Psalm 139:2 that God sees our thoughts afar off. Before we can even think a thought, God sees it. In verse 4 of that same Psalm, the Psalmist teaches that be-

fore we can even speak, God knows our words. Jesus taught that God knows what we have need of even before we ask Him (Matthew 6:8). The Hebrew writer wrote we must approach God in faith, recognizing He is God, and He rewards those who diligently seek Him (Hebrews 11:6). Consider the words of the Irishman Joseph Scriven,

> "What a Friend we have in Jesus, all our sins and griefs to bear.
> What a privilege to carry, everything to God in prayer.
> O what peace we often forfeit, O what needless pain we bear,
> All because we do not carry, everything to God in prayer."

Heralding this same truth, James, the brother of Jesus, taught in his epistle that we have not because we ask not (James 4:2b).

4. Suffering can be the result of reaping what one has sown. God's law of the harvest demands that we reap what we sow. This is not only true in agriculture, but it is true in the spiritual realm as well. For every cause, there is an effect. For every decision, there is a consequence. For every action, there is a result. When we sow to please the appetites or our flesh, we reap a crop of grief, disappointment, and corruption. However, reaping this bitter crop is not always immediate; and because of that, many individuals erroneously assume there will be no bitter crop for them to reap. These individuals fail to realize that sowing is done in one season, and reaping is done in another.

Eventually, everyone reaps what he or she has sown. Jesus taught that if God gives so much attention to the actions of a little sparrow, surely He gives greater attention to our actions and everything about us down to numbering the very hairs on our heads (Matthew 10:29-30). Not one of our deeds, whether good or bad, escapes the eyes of God. When we sow to please God, we reap a harvest of God's abundance (Hosea 8:7; and Galatians 6:7-8).

"Forgiveness is the fragrance the violet sheds on the heel that has crushed it." —*Mark Twain*

Mark Twain, born Samuel L. Clemens, was an American satirist, writer, humorist, and lecturer.

What about you? What kinds of seeds are you sowing? If as a believer, you have been guilty of sowing to the flesh and now desire God's forgiveness, remember that God delights in showing mercy to those who humble themselves (Micah 7:18). Please pray the following:

Dear heavenly Father, forgive me for sowing to my flesh. I desire Your cleansing and Your power in my life. Proverbs 21:1 teaches me that You have the power to turn even the hearts of kings in any direction You choose. I am asking that You turn my heart back to You. May any suffering I endure in the future from this day forward be the result of a righteous life and Your sovereign hand, and not the result of a disobedient walk before You. I ask these things in Jesus' name. Amen.

16

Empty Promises

A young man sat down and penned a love letter to his sweetheart who lived in a little town only fifty miles away. "Darling," he wrote, "If you only knew the depth of my love for you. You're always in my thoughts both day and night. You are the last thing on my mind before I fall asleep at night, and you are the first thing on my mind when I arise each morning. Knowing you love me too has made my life wonderful and exciting. I want you to know there is absolutely nothing or anyone in this world that could ever keep me from you."

The young man ended his letter, folded it, and placed it in the envelope. However, just before sealing it, he remembered something. Quickly extracting the letter from the envelope and unfolding it, he laid it out flatly upon the table surface. Picking up his pen he wrote at the bottom of his letter, "P.S. I almost forgot. Sorry I wasn't able to make it to your house the other night, but I really don't like driving in the rain."

A little rain surely put a big damper on this young man's promises of undying love and devotion to his sweetheart.

How much rain does it take to put a damper on our devotion and commitment to God? Professing to others our love and devotion to our Lord is one thing; however, our lives speak much louder to others than our words.

When all of our faith-talk lacks the corresponding faith-walk, our words become empty and meaningless to those who hear them. When true faith and devotion for our Lord is resident in our hearts, they will find a way to manifest themselves in and through our lives as believers.

Of course, some will argue that our good works alone cannot save us, and such an argument would certainly be true (Ephesians 2:9). However, the strongest evidence that any of us have that we are truly Christians before an unbelieving world is a life characterized by consistently good works (Ephesians 2:10).

Objecting to the works doctrine advocated by Jewish legalists, Paul declared that believers are justified in the sight of God by their faith alone (Ephesians 2:8-9).

Objecting to the unrestrained liberty and "live anyway you please" doctrine of those who preached license, James declared genuine believers who truly have faith in God through Jesus Christ are justified in the sight of men by their good works (James 2:17-26).

There is, of course, no disagreement between the writings of Paul and James on this matter. We are justified in the sight of God by our faith alone. Because we do not have the ability of God to see faith in our hearts (1 Samuel 16:7), good works, which are borne out of inner faith, justify us in the sight of men.

The Hebrew writer declares it is absolutely impossible for any of us to please God without faith (Hebrews 11:6). An individual's faith is the most crucial factor in his or her knowing God and being able to please Him.

It has been said every call to conversion is a call to discipleship. When our lives give unmistakable evidence that our faith in God is genuine, our words cease to be empty and meaningless to those who hear them.

"A faith that hasn't been tested cannot be trusted." — *Adrian Rogers*

Adrian Rogers was an American pastor, author, and three-term president of the Southern Baptist Convention.

What about you? Is your walking lining up with your talking? Does your life attract others to the God they see in you? If not, and you desire for Christ's light to shine in and through your life so that others may clearly see God in you, please pray the following:

> Dear heavenly Father, I desire for my life to honor You and bring glory to Your name. Help me to live a life that points others to Your beloved Son, Jesus Christ. Strengthen my faith and order my steps so that from this day forward my actions reflect the faith, the commitment, and the devotion I have in my heart for You. I ask these things in Jesus' name. Amen.

17

An Appointed Time

Long ago in a city named Troy, a man rushed to his friend's house in the heat of the day and pleaded with his friend to let him borrow a horse to escape to a nearby city.

"For heaven's sake, man, what has frightened you so?" his friend asked the terrified man.

"I just saw Death standing and staring strangely at me in the marketplace!"

"How can you be sure it was him?" his friend inquired.

"Years ago, an old wise man told me how I could recognize him!"

After describing what he saw, the terrified man again pleaded with his friend to loan him a horse to make his escape. His friend graciously agreed, and off the frightened man rode as hard as he could to a town called Smyrna, where he was confident he would be safe.

The friend, still somewhat skeptical, rushed down to the marketplace in hopes of finding this character his terrified friend had described as Death. After pushing and shoving his way through the crowd for several minutes, he spotted a tall man in a robe. His garment covered his head, but his face was exposed.

He immediately rushed forward through the crowd to confront the tall stranger. "Are you really Death?"

To his surprise the stranger looked directly at him and answered, "I am."

"Well, you truly frightened a good friend of mine earlier when he spotted you here in this marketplace. He said when he saw you, you were staring strangely at him."

"I'm afraid I was," Death answered. "It really surprised me to see your friend here today in Troy. You see, I have an appointment with him this evening in Smyrna!"

Scripture declares,

And as it is appointed unto men once to die, but after this the judgment (Hebrews 9:27).

Death is as much a reality as life itself. Unfortunately, many individuals choose to ignore this fact unto the very truth of it stands staring them in the face.

Ignoring our inevitable appointment with death in no way disrupts his schedule. Death is a divinely appointed chauffeur, who may arrive early for an appointment but never late. His job is to transport his passengers from the physical realm to the spiritual realm where judgment awaits them.

Nothing could be more sobering or chilling than to look death in the face and see his cold gaze fixed on you. Death has no favorites. Death makes no exceptions. Death keeps his appointments with both the young and the old, the rich and the poor, the male and the female, the happy and the sad, the intelligent and the ignorant, those famous and those unknown, the friend and the foe, the hungry and the filled, those free and those incarcerated, and those healthy and those sick.

An Appointed Time

All who breathe have an appointed time with death. Death is never more than a heartbeat, a breath, a word, a whisper, or a sigh away. He busies himself with his scheduled appointments from the earliest morning hours before the break of day to the latest midnight hours, meeting with those who sleep never to awaken in this life again. To most he is that unwanted guest, that daytime rambler—that midnight creeper.

Death has an appointment with each of us, and barring divine intervention, there is no delaying our meeting with him. No one misses Death's meetings, shows up late, dresses inappropriately, cancels, or reschedules any of Death's meetings to a more convenient time. There is no more convenient time than the one already appointed with him. We can run, but we cannot hide behind wealth, healthy lifestyles, happiness, power, friends, or pleasure, from this dark knight.

From the very moment an individual is born, Death takes the sand glass of time, turns it upside down, and hangs it around the neck of the new arrival. For some, the sand flows slowly; for others, the sand flows quickly. However, for everyone, the sand flows continuously. Yes, from the time of our birth into this world, we begin our pilgrimage to our appointed time with Death. For the believer, Death is our escort to the heavenly bliss that awaits us. For the nonbeliever, Death is the grim reaper.

Scripture teaches if we are born once, we will die twice—physical death in this world and spiritual or eternal death before the Great White Throne judgment of God (Revelation 20:11-15). Scripture also teaches if we are born twice (John 3:3-17), we will die only once—physical death not the eternal death (John 8:51). For those of us who place our hope and trust in Jesus Christ, our first encounter with Death will be our only encounter with Death.

For those who choose not to place their hope and trust in Jesus Christ, they will face this dreaded reaper twice. Ironically most nonbelievers fear death more than they do God's judgment, which awaits them, so it is extremely important that we prayerfully share the liberating message of the gospel of Jesus Christ with nonbelievers around us.

The best any of us can do is to plant a gospel seed in the life of a nonbeliever or water a gospel seed that has already been planted by some other believer and then trust God to give the increase. However, for those nonbelievers who continually reject the gospel message and choose instead to die in their sins at their appointed time with Death, these individuals await a judgment described by the late Dr. D. James Kennedy, former Senior Pastor of the Coral Ridge Presbyterian Church in Fort Lauderdale, Florida as "…[a judgment] for which there shall be no escape, a verdict for which there will be no appeal, and a sentence for which there will be no parole."

"Many who plan to seek God at the eleventh hour die at 10:30." —*Author Unknown*.

What about you today? Are you sharing the gospel message with those who are perishing around you? If not and you desire God to give you the power and courage to do so, please pray the following:

> Dear heavenly Father, I realize the harvest is great and the laborers are few. I ask Your forgiveness for not having been more diligent and faithful to the work

An Appointed Time

You have called and empowered me to do. Touch my heart, O God, in such a way that others around me will be impacted by how I live. From this day forward give me a burden for lost souls and help me to remember that I too was once a lost soul until someone shared the glorious, liberating message of Jesus Christ with me. I ask these things in Jesus' name. Amen.

18

A Hiker, a Ledge, and a Voice

A hiker was making his way along a cliff in the mountains one dark, chilly night when all of a sudden, his foot slipped. As he began falling, he quickly reached out, grabbed a ledge, and held onto it with all his might. He hung there in the deep darkness under a moonless and starless night for minutes, struggling desperately with all his strength to pull himself upward to safer ground, but nothing he tried worked. Minutes continued to tick away and exhaustion began to set in. His fingers, which clung tightly to the ledge, grew numb and his entire body grew weaker. He prayed for more strength but grew weaker instead.

Finally, he screamed as loud as he could, "Hey, is there anyone up there who can help me? Help! Help! Can anyone hear me?"

Suddenly a voice from above whispered, "Let go!"

The weakened hiker looked up and saw no one. He looked down and saw only darkness. He ignored the voice, and again shouted, "Is there anyone up there who can help me?" This time there was no response to his appeal. Within minutes the muscles in his body began agonizing with excruciating pain. He cried out again, "Dear, God, please, please, help me!"

Again, the voice he had heard earlier, he now heard again.

A Hiker, a Ledge, and a Voice

"Just let go," the voice said, repeating the earlier command. And just as before, the hiker, seeing no one, ignored the voice. However, within a few more minutes, weariness and muscle fatigue finally overtook him, and he screamed aloud as he released his grip, only to drop safely in the darkness to a ledge only three feet below him.

When was the last time we had a ledge experience and were afraid to let go and trust the still small voice of God? Ledge experiences are uniquely different for each of us because each one is designed with you and me in mind. Such experiences make us feel off balance and uneasy with our spiritual footing. We feel as though we have been left dangling in the dark, and so we struggle desperately to get back to our comfort zones, the places where we feel most secure.

However, ledge experiences in our lives as believers are absolutely essential. Without them we tend to become self-reliant, sometimes even self-centered, and spiritually comfortable. These experiences remind us of just how utterly helpless and totally dependent on God we really are. Go ahead and admit it—we all need to be reminded from time to time. Our ledge experiences tend to lift our spiritual gaze from the horizontal upwards to the vertical where it belongs.

Unfortunately, we all live in a hustle and bustle world that wreaks havoc in our lives because of demanding schedules. The more demanding our schedules become, the more the spiritual disciplines we have developed tend to suffer. If we are not careful, we find ourselves being hurried about at such a rapid pace that we rarely slow down long enough to check with God about anything and listen to that still small voice.

At least that seems to be the case until we find ourselves feeling totally helpless due to some health, job, or family crisis. During these totally helpless periods in our lives, when the pace has been slowed or stopped altogether, we become all ears for the voice of God and have a ledge experience. Ledge experiences tend to take us by surprise, force us to reassess our priorities, and leave us open to the voice of God where we give Him our totally undivided attention.

Consider the hiker's prayer and the response of God in the story. The hiker could have experienced relief much sooner if he had been willing to listen and obey the still small voice of God. Using God as a last resort is bad enough (Matthew 6:33) but disobeying Him once He has revealed His will to us only invites needless suffering in our lives. Sometimes our greatest difficulty is not in discovering God's will but in accepting it.

Consider the prophet Jonah. Discovering God's will was not Jonah's challenge (Jonah 1:1-2) but performing it was (Jonah 1:3). Just as God orchestrated circumstances in Jonah's life to get his attention and obedience, God can orchestrate ledge experiences in our lives to get our attention and obedience as well.

As believers we all know God is sovereign, and all things are ultimately subject to Him. Knowing this already, why would we as believers deliberately disobey His revealed will for our lives? Let's look at two reasons:

1. Like Jonah, after discovering God's will, we simply do not want to do it. Of course, taking this position reveals how we have lost our spiritual perspective. Our gaze has

become fixed upon the horizontal things of life—what I want, what makes me happy, what I would like to accomplish, what my plans are, etc. Do you recognize the I, me, and my in those desires? Our thinking tends to erode to this state when we neglect to carve out time in our busy schedules for personal devotion and Bible study on a regular basis. We find ourselves forgetting our lives and our bodies are no longer our own. Why? Because we willingly signed up to be bondservants of the Lord Jesus Christ (1 Corinthians 6:19-20).

Slaves have no rights. As believers, our rights were nailed to the cross at Calvary. Our willful disobedience to the revealed will of God for our lives eventually invites God's intervention by way of His chastening hand Hebrew 12:5-6; 1 Corinthians 11:31-32). We force God to bring about circumstances which lovingly, yet painfully, bring our spiritual perspective and eyes vertical and fixed again on our Savior, the Author and Finisher of our faith (Hebrews 12:1-2a).

2. We are fearful to move forward from our comfort zone into the unknown. Fear tends to incapacitate us and keep us from moving forward spiritually as Christians. To fear is to be uncertain about God's plans for our lives. If we find ourselves desperately hanging and clinging onto our comfort zones while ignoring the voice of God urging us to let go, it just could be we have not come to the place in our spiritual walk where we truly trust that God has our best interests at heart. John, the Apostle, wrote,

There is no fear in love; perfect love casteth out fear; because fear hath torment [has to do with punishment].

He that feareth is not made perfect in love (1 John 4:18).

To be perfected in God's love is to come to the realization of how much He truly loves and cares for us. It is to understand that God is not going to allow anything to happen to us except what is for our good and to His glory (Romans 8:28-29).

Even death itself only serves to usher us into His glorious presence (2 Corinthians 5:8). When we come to an awareness of just how great His love is for us, our fear is dispelled, and with absolute assurance we can say, "My life is in God's hands, no matter what."

Each of us needs to become more sensitive and obedient to the still small voice of God in our lives. If we will be diligent to cultivate intimacy with Him through regular worship, personal devotion, and Bible study, then when life's footing becomes unstable, we will experience the security and comfort He alone provides.

"Faith never knows where it is being led, but it loves and knows the One who is leading." —*Oswald Chambers*

Oswald Chambers was a prominent early twentieth century Scottish Protestant Christian minister and teacher.

What about you? Do your circumstances have you dangling in the dark—clinging desperately to the edge of your comfort zone while ignoring the still small voice of God to let go and trust Him? If so, and you sincerely desire to trust God in your circumstances, please pray the following:

A Hiker, a Ledge, and a Voice

Dear heavenly Father, saying I trust You in all things is a lot easier than actually doing so. Help my unbelief. Dispel my fear and rid me of my feelings of uncertainty about Your sovereign plan for my life. I desire only that which You have already ordained for me, and having said this, I desire to be perfected in Your love from this day forward. I ask these things in Jesus' name. Amen.

19

Remembering to Love

A Raisin in the Sun is a play written by Lorraine Hansberry, which debuted on Broadway in 1959. Drawing upon experiences in her own life growing up in Chicago's Woodlawn neighborhood, the play depicts a poor black family's struggle to rise above social barriers and their economic condition in hopes of securing a brighter future.

The love this aging mother and her two grown children have for one another becomes sorely tested by the son's lust for money and power. The mother had just received a reasonably large sum of insurance money following her husband's death. Her plans were to use part of the money to finance a college education for Beneatha, her daughter. The balance she intended to use as a down payment on a better house she intended to purchase in a white neighborhood. A group of white homeowners in the neighborhood soon discovered the family's plans and sent a representative to offer the family money to look elsewhere for a new house. Their offer greatly insulted the quick-tempered, rude-talking Beneatha.

The mother had entrusted most of the insurance money to her son Walter to deposit in the bank for safekeeping. However, Walter secretly had his own plans for the money. Motivated by his greed, he allowed himself to be talked into a get-rich-quick scheme by a con man named Willie and his associates. It wasn't very long before Walter discovered his so-called business partners had skipped town, taking his mother's money with them. When his mother and Beneatha discovered the painful truth about Walter's deceit, they were devastated. Walter's actions not only ruined Beneatha's immediate educational plans but the family's hopes of moving into a better home as well.

Frustrated, tearful, and angry about a plan gone sour, Walter intended to retaliate by accepting the money offered to them by the unsuspecting white homeowners as though the family still intended to move. Casting all self-respect and dignity aside, Walter dramatically crawled about on the floor on hands and knees before his sister Beneatha and his mother, illustrating to them how he intended to act in the presence of the white homeowners as he dishonestly took their money. His dramatization infuriated Beneatha, who turned to her mother and scoffed as she pointed her condemning finger at Walter,

Beneatha turned to her mother and scoffed—insisting her brother Walter was no man but a pathetic imitation of one. Brokenhearted, her mother turned to her daughter and expressed disappointment over what now seemed like nothing more than shattered hopes. She further expressed disappointment not only over Walter's greed, which left him vulnerable to con-men, but to Beneatha's surprise—over Beneatha's self-righteous attitude, which blinded this young lady to her own absence of compassion and love for her brother.

Beneatha stubbornly retorted Walter was no longer her brother. Her mother quickly rebuked her for writing her brother off as being unredeemable.

Hurt, Beneatha appealed to her mother to understand her

point of view, insisting her mother and deceased father had taught her to despise any man who was void of dignity and self-respect, not only for others but for himself as well. And since the shoe fit—that meant her brother Walther as well.

Her mother acknowledged that she and her late husband had indeed raised Beneatha to despise an individual who exhibited no dignity and respect for himself or others, but she wisely added that they had also taught Beneatha something else—to love her brother.

Have we known a spiritual brother like Walter, who has really blown it? How did we react toward him? Were we harsh and unyielding, or were we gentle and forgiving? Let's take a look at what Paul was inspired to write to the believers in the various cities of Galatia, regarding this matter:

> *Brethren, if a man be overtaken* [caught] *in a fault* [trespass or sin], *ye which are spiritual, restore such an one in the spirit of meekness; considering thyself, lest thou also be tempted* (Galatians 6:1).

Paul is saying in this verse if a brother has been caught committing a sin, only those whose lives exhibit the characteristics of the fruit of the Spirit (Galatians 5:22-23) and the filling of the Spirit (Ephesians 5:18), should gently confront the sinning brother. Those confronting him should do so with an attitude of humility, recognizing they too, if it were not for the grace of God, could fall into sin.

It is so easy to be a backseat driver, sitting there critiquing someone else's driving against the standard of our own. It is easy to sit comfortably on our sofas watching our favorite fighter on television and criticizing him for not ducking when he should have or punching when his opponent was open. It is also easy to look at the faults in another person and detest the weaknesses we see.

However, if we are honest about it, there have been times when we were at the steering wheel of a car and made driving mistakes. There were those times when we were growing up and had to fight the little bully Johnny, and we simply did not duck in time, and our shiny, bruised eye let everyone know it. And, there have been times, when the very best of us committed sin, and when we did, we begged God for forgiveness and were so thankful and humbled that He did not send a lynch mob for us.

Why is it when our shoes are on someone else's feet, they look bigger? Why do we get so offended when we discover a particular person has criticized us, when we have repeatedly criticized others ourselves? Why is it that when the very sin we have committed and been forgiven for is committed by someone else, it seems much worse than when we did it?

The word self-righteousness comes to mind. It is an attitude we should really avoid at all cost. Paul wrote to these same believers,

> *Let us not be desirous of vain glory* [conceited], *provoking one another, envying one another* (Galatians 5:26).

In the fifth chapter of the book of Galatians Paul encourages believers to live and walk in the Spirit (Galatians 5:16; 25) and to exhibit by their very lives the characteristics of a Spirit-filled life (Galatians 5:22-23). He contrasted this mindset with individuals who choose to be conceited, self-righteous and envious of those who have what they lack.

Therefore when Paul is saying in Galatians 6:1 only those

who are spiritual should gently confront the sinning brother, he is excluding the individuals he described in Galatians 5:26. Why? Because the spiritually minded under the control of the Holy Spirit are a lot better equipped in restoring the sinning brother to fellowship than the self-righteous, who feel they are better than half the believers they know and envious of the other half.

When a brother or a sister is caught committing a sin, those who gently confront the individual should do at least five things:

1. Pray earnestly before confronting, pray earnestly while confronting, and pray earnestly after confronting.
2. Assure the individual you are there only to help, not to criticize.
3. Tactfully and in humility point out or remind the individual about the gravity of his or her sin.
4. Encourage the individual to repent and seek the Lord's forgiveness.
5. Be willing to pray with him or her during your meeting if he or she is willing.

Too few of us are interceding on behalf of a struggling brother or sister in the faith. As Christians we all believe in the power of intercessory prayer; however, many of us tend to think it is someone else's responsibility to do it. Paul encourages spiritually minded believers to not behave like those who are self-righteous, conceited, and envious, but to come alongside a struggling brother or sister and prop him or her up and support them. Why? Because in doing so, we demonstrate the love of Jesus Christ (Galatians 6:2). To do less mars the testimony of the church before the world. Don Baker, noted pastor and author, in his book entitled *Beyond Forgiveness,* writes, "The church is the only army in the world that has the reputation for deserting its wounded."

Beneatha was quick to remember what she had learned about detesting deceit but slow to remember what she had been taught about love and forgiveness.

What about us? Are we quick to remember the things we should be forgetting and forgetting the things we should be remembering?

God does not reject us, His children, because we make mistakes. If He did, not one of us would ever see heaven. He is not only the God of second chances, but He is the God of infinite chances. Remember, Jesus' words regarding forgiveness—seventy times seven (Matthew 18:21-22). If God is the God of infinite chances, and He is, how should we be who follow Him and call ourselves His disciples?

> "Whatever a person may be like, we must still love them because we love God." —*John Calvin*
>
> John Calvin was a French Protestant theologian during the Protestant Reformation. He was the primary developer of the theology on Christianity known as Calvinism.

If your attitude and behavior has eliminated opportunities for you to be used within the body of believers as a spiritual minded Christian, and you now desire to be used of God in that way, tell Him so. Please pray the following:

> Dear heavenly Father, I know You can see our hearts while others are limited to seeing only our actions. I

know that my heart has not been totally surrendered to You in the past, and for that I am deeply sorry. Forgive me and cleanse me of this sin. I surrender both my heart and my life to You and Your service from this day forward. Give me the kind of heart You refer to as perfect, which Your Word speaks of in 2 Chronicles 16:9. Help me to never again be self-righteous but walk in humility before You and love and encourage each of my brothers and sisters in the Lord. I ask these things in Jesus' name. Amen.

20

A Broken Will

In the ever-popular American saga *Roots*, written by renowned author Alex Haley, an incident occurs where Kunta Kinte, a slave boy from the continent of Africa, is strung up by his arms and beaten because of his refusal to acknowledge or answer to his new American slave name Toby. Toby was the name assigned to him by his slave owner. When this saga moved from the pages of Haley's book to the television screen in the homes of millions of viewers, both white and black Americans alike sat horrified as they witnessed a young slave boy being brutally whipped because of his obstinacy and unwillingness to surrender his will to that of his master. Repeatedly the whip cracked as it tore skin and drew blood from Kunta's back. Between each crack of the whip, the foreman stopped and gave Kunta an opportunity to acknowledge "Toby" as his new name.

When Kunta would hang there silent, the foreman would demand this young slave boy acknowledge aloud his name was now Toby, the name given to him by his owner.

But repeatedly Kunta would stubbornly hang there, insisting his name was Kunta Kinte. Despite the excruciating pain and humiliation, he was suffering in the presence of onlookers, including other slaves, the young slave tenaciously continued, despite several opportunities to do otherwise, to

If the Shoe Fits

insist his name was Kunta. With each of his refusals to acknowledge his new slave name came the slashing of the foreman's whip across his already scarred and bloodied back.

Standing nearby in the crowd was an old wise slave named Fiddler. Fiddler had forewarned young Kunta that his rebellious attitude would cost him dearly, but Kunta chose to ignore Fiddler's wise counsel. Knowing all this could have been avoided still gave Fiddler no comfort as he stood helplessly watching the young slave being brutally whipped. Fiddler did the only thing he could do. He whispered a prayer that God would give this stubborn young slave boy enough wisdom to surrender to his master's will before the foreman would be forced to whip him to death.

Finally, after many brutal slashes, the foreman's whip was suddenly silenced. As he had done several times before, the slave owner asked the young slave to publicly acknowledge his name.

Kunta finally whispered, amid tears and a broken body which hung limply in the presence of a sympathetic crowd, that his name was Toby.

Captured in 1767 by slave traders in the small West African country of Gambia and transported to America on a slave ship, Kunta Kinte, a member of the Mandinka tribe, suffered a harsh awakening when his slave master forced him to realize that change was going to be an integral part of his new life in America. Essentially, his master wanted Kunta to die to all the things that were once native to him in Africa, including his African birth name, Kunta Kinte.

A Broken Will

However, Kunta's repeated refusal to do so forced his master to resort to measures that, although painful, were effective in breaking the will of this stubborn, young slave. As Christians we too are slaves—spiritual slaves, but not involuntarily as in the case of Kunta Kinté. We became slaves willingly. We understand that God purchased us at a tremendous cost to Himself—the blood of His Son, the Lord Jesus Christ (1 Corinthians 6:20).

We are not our own—we are God's property, and because we are, God has given us a new name. We are no longer to be called sinners but rather saints. As saints, our Master calls us to die to all those things that were once normal and native to us (Romans 6:11) prior to our salvation experience and to live our new lives in a manner that glorifies Him (Matthew 5:16).

To the Christians in Rome, Paul wrote,

For whether we live, we live unto the Lord; whether we die we die unto the Lord; whether we live therefore, or die, we are the Lord's (Romans 14:8).

In the book of Acts, Luke, the beloved physician, records an incident involving a Pharisee named Saul, who hunted and persecuted Christians. Accompanied by others, Saul, with letters in his possession from the high priest addressed to the synagogues in Damascus, was in hot pursuit of Christians on the Damascus Road when suddenly he encountered a blinding light that caused him to fall from his horse. Looking up Saul heard a voice saying:

Saul, Saul, why persecutest thou Me? And he said, Who art thou, Lord? And the Lord said, I am Jesus whom thou persecutest; it is hard for thee to kick against the pricks. And he trembling and astonished said, Lord, what wilt Thou have me to do? (Acts 9:4-6a)

Also, in the very next chapter, Luke records another incident involving the Apostle Peter, which took place on a housetop in Joppa, an old port city on the Mediterranean Sea. Around noon Peter went up to the roof of the house to pray. While there he became very hungry, and as the meal was being prepared inside the house below, Peter fell into a trance.

> *And* [Peter] *saw heaven opened, and a certain vessel (canvas; sheet) descending unto him, as it had been a great sheet knit at the four corners, and let down to the earth. Wherein were all manner of four-footed beasts of the earth, and wild beasts, and creeping things, and fowls of the air. And there came a voice to him, Rise, Peter, kill and eat. But Peter said, Not so, Lord; for I have never eaten any thing that is common or unclean* (Acts 10:11-14).

Notice the contrast in these two accounts. One of these men was saying, yes, Lord, and the other was saying no, Lord. If we are truly God's property, and if we are no longer our own, then how can we as Christians say no? The very term "Lord" means God has total authority, control, and power over our lives. As Lord, He is our master, our chief, and our ruler. Can that which is owned rightfully say no to its owner?

When you and I refuse to surrender certain areas of our will to the Lordship of Jesus Christ, immediately the Holy Spirit, like the wise old Fiddler in the story, begins to nudge us and lovingly warn us through other believers, God's Word, prayer, and even through our circumstances to obey our heavenly Master's voice. Why? Because He wants only what is best for us, and He knows that if we will heed His gentle

A Broken Will

warnings, we will save ourselves from needless suffering in this life.

However, if as Christians we persist in resisting the counsel of our Lord's still small voice, we may force Him to bring about circumstances in our lives specifically designed to break our will and render us submissive to His sovereign purpose for us as individuals (1 Corinthians 11:29-30).

> "Just as a servant knows that he must first obey his master in all things, so the surrender to an implicit and unquestionable obedience must become the essential characteristic of our lives." —*Andrew Murray*

Andrew Murray was the child of Dutch Reformed Church missionaries from Scotland, who became a Christian pastor in South Africa.

What about you? Have you surrendered every area of your heart and life to His lordship? If not, but you desire to, tell Him. Please pray the following:

> Dear heavenly Father, please forgive me for my stubbornness and unwillingness to daily surrender myself totally to Your lordship. I now realize that when I invited Jesus Christ into my heart as my Savior, there were areas in my life that up to this point I had never surrendered to the lordship of Jesus Christ. Forgive me. Cleanse me of this sin of disobedience, and from this day forward, please give me a heart and a life that is daily and totally surrendered to Your lordship. I ask these things in Jesus' name. Amen.

21

A Father, a Son, and an Issue of Discipline

A father was at home with his ten-year-old son Johnny while his wife shopped. Johnny asked his father if he could go outside and play in the yard. His father granted him permission on the condition that Johnny stay in their yard and steer clear of Tommy, the neighbors' mischievous little boy.

Despite his father's warning, Johnny eventually strayed from their yard and began playing with Tommy next door. Before long the two began arguing and then fighting. Johnny's father overheard Tommy's mother shouting at the two from her window. He jumped up from his seat, rushed to the back door, and swung it open. Spotting the two little boys fighting in the neighbor's yard, Johnny's dad rushed forward into the yard headed for the two.

When the boys spotted Johnny's father approaching, they immediately stopped fighting. Tommy ran into his house, and Johnny raced back to his own yard. Johnny's father ran up to Johnny and firmly took his son by the arm, marching him back into their house.

"Why did you disobey me, Johnny?" his father asked, visibly upset with his son.

"But, Daddy, I didn't."

A Father, a Son, and an Issue of Discipline

"Oh, but you did. Did I not tell you to stay in our yard and leave Tommy alone?"

"Yes, sir, but I did."

"Listen, Johnny, I saw you with my own eyes fighting Tommy in his yard. You are lying."

"No, Daddy. I was playing in our yard just like you told me. And, Tommy asked me to come play with him, and I told him no. So he came into our yard and drug me over to his yard and started fighting me."

The father looked into his son's eyes. Johnny's expression said it all. "Son, you are lying to me!"

"No, sir, Daddy, I'm not lying."

"Yes, you are. What did you learn in Sunday school about what the Bible says about lying?"

Little Johnny dropped his head and thought momentarily about the discipline he could possibly receive and then timidly looked up into his father eyes and said, "It says it's an abomination, but a mighty present help in time of trouble!"

The Hebrews writer wrote,

My son, despise not thou the chastening of the Lord, nor faint when thou art rebuked of Him. For whom the Lord loveth He chasteneth, and scourgeth every son whom He receiveth. If ye endure chastening, God dealeth with you, as with sons; for what son is he whom the father chasteneth not? But if ye be without chastisement, whereof all are partakers, then are ye bastards, and not sons (Hebrews 12:5b-8).

Which father shows the greater love—the one who allows his child to do whatever his child desires, even if what the child does is not good for him or her, or the father who lovingly disciplines and corrects his child, knowing that in doing so he is steering his child in the right direction?

Johnny's father represents the latter. He was about to discipline Johnny because he loved his son and wanted Johnny to learn a valuable lesson regarding authority and obedience. Likewise, God's discipline, which can take the form of trials and suffering in believers' lives, is proof He loves us, and we are His children. Hebrews 12:5-8 is quoting Proverbs 3:11-12 in order to help believers understand that God uses discipline in our lives as a means of training and educating us.

Both Hebrews and Proverbs passages articulate the type of reactions we as believers may have in response to the discipline of God in our lives. Proverbs articulates two possible reactions while Hebrews articulates the same two but adds a third possible reaction, which is recommended over the previous two.

Despising divine chastisement—either completely disregarding it altogether or taking God's discipline lightly—is the first reaction some believers have toward God's discipline in their personal lives. To faint or become weary by becoming discouraged or losing heart and giving up is the second reaction some believers have to God's discipline in their personal lives.

Hebrews 12:7 provides a third and preferred reaction toward God's discipline in our personal lives—to endure it. We need to submit to His discipline and learn the valuable spiritual lessons God is teaching us through it. God's discipline may come in many forms. It may come in the form of loss of

A Father, a Son, and an Issue of Discipline

income, health issues, persecution, or broken relationships, just to name a few. However, no matter what form divine discipline takes in our lives, when we endure it, we learn the valuable lessons God is attempting to teach us and become better equipped for ministry.

Jesus warned Peter that Satan desired to sift Peter as wheat (Luke 22:31). It was Satan's desire to crush Peter just as he had been allowed to crush and sift Job (Job 1:9-12). Wheat was sifted to remove chaff, withered grains, and dirt. While it is true that God tempts no man to do evil (James 1:13), it is also true God allows us to endure the temptations of the devil in order that our strengths and weaknesses—the chaff, withered grains, and dirt in our lives may be revealed. In short, God allows us to be sifted for service.

Consider Paul's words to the church at Rome:

We glory in tribulation also; knowing that tribulation worketh patience; and patience, experience [character]; *and experience, hope; and hope maketh not ashamed; because the love of God is shed abroad in our hearts by the Holy Ghost which is given unto us* (Romans 5:3-5).

Paul is not saying that as believers we should look forward to heartache, pain, and suffering. Rather, Paul is saying when we as believers find ourselves going through periods like that, we should rejoice in the midst of this suffering, not because we enjoy it but because we know through these things God is teaching us perseverance. Perseverance builds character and gives us greater hope in God's plan for our lives.

Paul could speak from personal experience. God had given him a thorn in his flesh (2 Corinthians 12:7-10). After seeking the Lord about this matter on three separate occasions and requesting it be removed, Paul said God spoke to Him and helped him understand His grace was sufficient for Paul. Why? It is because God's strength and power would be most effective in Paul's weakness. What was Paul's reaction to this revelation? Paul wrote,

> *Most gladly therefore will I rather glory in my infirmities that the power of Christ may rest upon me. Therefore, I take pleasure in infirmities, in reproaches, in necessities, in precautions, in distresses for Christ's sake; for when I am weak; then am I strong* (2 Corinthians 12:9b-10).

In Malachi 3:17 God promises blessings to those who fear and reverence Him. Concerning them God says,

> *They shall be Mine, saith the Lord of hosts, in that day when I make up My jewels* (Malachi 3:17).

This is the scripture, which William O. Cushing had in mind in 1856 when he developed the words to the song entitled, "When He Cometh." George F. Root later added the music to Cushing's words in 1866. Cushing wrote,

> When He cometh, when He cometh
> To make up His jewels,
> All His jewels, precious jewels,
> His loved and His own.
>
> Like the stars of the morning,
> His brightness adorning,
> They shall shine in their beauty,
> Bright gems for His crown.

A Father, a Son, and an Issue of Discipline

He will gather, He will gather
The gems for His kingdom;
All the pure ones, all the bright ones,
His loved and His own.

Little children, little children,
Who love their Redeemer
Are the jewels, precious jewels,
His loved and His own.

Borrowing from these scriptures and this song, Joni Eareckson Tada wrote,

"The stones that were fit for the temple were all dressed in the quarry. There was not a sound of chisel or hammer at the site of the temple. And down here on earth is all the chiseling and the hammering and the honing and the shaping and the refining and the polishing, but our sufferings fit us to be jewels in His crown."

What about us? How are we reacting to God's discipline in our lives? Are we despising it? Are we losing heart and becoming discouraged by it? Or, are we enduring it as Paul, who encouraged us as believers to do likewise. To willingly endure God's discipline is to understand that God is using it to correct, educate, and train us into becoming a more usable vessel for His great work of redemption in the lives of those around us.

"Smooth seas do not make skillful sailors." —*Author unknown*

If you have been reacting poorly to God's disciplining hand in your life, and you desire to experience His wisdom and power in helping you respond properly to His discipline, tell Him so. Please pray the following:

> Dear heavenly Father, thank You for loving me enough to discipline me. As Your child, I want to thank You for correcting me, training me, and guiding me in the right direction. As the Psalmist prayed in Psalm 119:133, I also pray that You order my steps in Your word that iniquity not have dominion in my life. You know what is best for me, and I submit to Your sovereign plan for my life and ask that You to give me discernment, wisdom, and power to endure any trials and suffering You allow to come my way. Please help me to remember that divine discipline always works out ultimately for my good and to Your glory. I ask these things in Jesus' name. Amen.

22

A Sign, a Warning, and the Undiscerning

When I was in the military serving in a medical unit, our most frequent activity was to conduct physical examinations and maintain medical records of all enlisted personnel. I recall an incident that required us to contact one particular soldier and have him report for more testing. His x-ray had revealed a spot on his lung. I recall it so vividly because this particular soldier had a very outgoing and jovial personality. He worked in the mess hall and laughed and carried on a lot with people who were there to eat. There was no ignoring his presence. If he was around, everyone knew it.

There was something else about him, he always had a half-cigar crammed tightly in the right corner of his mouth, whether it was lit or not. He never took the cigar out even when he was talking, laughing, and joking. Like a permanent fixture, the half-cigar set perched upon his bottom lip, as much at home as the tongue in his mouth.

When our unit notified him a spot appeared on his x-ray, he returned to the medical dispensary where I worked and submitted to another x-ray. After being x-rayed a second time, he was asked to take a seat out front while he waited. He sat within six feet of my desk, which was covered with the forms our enlisted personnel were required to complete prior to submitting to a physical or special examination. As he sat waiting for the results of the second x-ray, his face revealed the anxiety he was feeling within. There was no half-cigar protruding from his lips, no jovial smile upon his face, and no joking or laughing with anyone present. In fact, the other soldiers entering the dispensary barely got a grunt from him in response to their greetings. As he continued to wait for the results, a look of fear, uncertainty, and helplessness settled upon his countenance. I tried talking to him to get his mind off what could possibly be more bad news, but he was in no talking mood. I wondered to myself what I would be thinking if I were he sitting there waiting on the second x-ray results. Would I be praying, repenting? What? Was he reflecting back over his life? Was he pleading with his Creator for a second chance? I wondered.

Finally, the x-ray technician arrived out front in the waiting room of the medical dispensary and informed the anxious soldier his x-ray results were good. The technician explained the spot on his previous x-ray had been a flaw in the film. Hearing the news, the soldier smiled broadly, pulled a half-cigar from his shirt pocket and shoved it into the corner of his mouth, stood to his feet, thanked the technician, and left. I saw him on the base several times after this incident, and he, with his half-cigar protruding from his mouth, was as carefree, jovial, and joking as always.

However, about two-and-a-half to three months after this incident in the medical dispensary, the same soldier got into a very heated argument with his elderly neighbor in their apartment building. Apparently the two had argued in the past, and there was no love between them. The arguments

A Sign, a Warning, and the Undiscerning

were ignited by the soldier's continual insistence on playing his music so loudly it irritated his elderly neighbor who lived next to his apartment. On this particular evening, the old man repeatedly demanded the soldier turn his music down. The soldier repeatedly refused and another heated argument ensued in the doorway of the soldier's apartment. The elderly man stormed off to his apartment, secured a firearm, and returned to the soldier's apartment. When the soldier answered the doorbell, the elderly man fired a shot, fatally wounding him. The soldier slumped to his knees, and within moments he was dead.

God's signs and warnings may sometimes come to us in the form of a spot on an x-ray. Such times force us, or should, to conduct a self-inventory of our lives and our lifestyles and to assess where we stand or not stand with God. These signs and warnings can come in the form of a health crisis, a near-death experience, a loss of financial freedom brought on by unexpected debt, or the death of someone close. No matter how they come, each is specifically designed to get our attention, whether our spiritual walk is one of obedience or disobedience before our Lord. No matter what our standing is before Him, at any time the sovereign God reserves the right to get our attention.

When we experience an unusual occurrence, which could be a divine sign or warning, it behooves us to go to God in prayer, asking, "Lord, what would You have me to learn from this experience? What are You teaching me?" It could very well be God is growing us spiritually through this experience, increasing our faith and trust in Him, or He could be dealing with sin in our lives and our need to repent. Either way, for the believer God's signs and warnings are designed to ultimately work for our good and to His glory (Romans 8:28).

If we are nonbelievers, God gives us a sense of longing, of emptiness, the feeling something is missing in our life so that no matter what we do or accomplish, we do not have any lasting fulfillment. There is that ever so continually subtle gnawing at our conscience. It is like going to the refrigerator in the late evening because we are hungry and thirsty for something, but we just do not know for what. As we stand there gazing into a refrigerator filled with food and refreshments, we reach for nothing because no food or drink we see will satisfy our hunger or quench our thirst. Therefore, we close the refrigerator and remain hungry and thirsty for what, we still do not know.

Spiritual hunger and thirst work the very same way. There is a longing within us when we are nonbelievers for something. We may not know what that something is, but we know it is real. An emptiness begins to grow within us, and we become increasing more dissatisfied with things that cannot satisfy our spiritual hunger or quench our spiritual thirst. Why? It is because God has created within each of us a God-sized vacuum that He and He alone can fill. We have a throne within each of our hearts that He and He alone should occupy.

How do most of us as nonbelievers respond to this inner longing deep within us? Many of us attempt to fill this emptiness or void with the lures and enticements of the world—fortune, fame, power, and pleasure. We convince ourselves that if we enjoy these things in abundance, the empti-

A Sign, a Warning, and the Undiscerning

ness will go away. In reality these lures do tend to satisfy us initially but only for a very short season, and then the emptiness—the inner longing—returns. Why? It is because emptiness is to the soul what pain is to the body—it tells us something is wrong.

Regarding this inner longing of man for God, Solomon wrote,

> *He* [God] *has also set eternity in the hearts of men* (Ecclesiastes 3:11).

Solomon's insightful and inspired words reveal to us that we will never be completely satisfied with the temporal things of this world. Within each of our hearts, God has placed an inner longing for more than this earthly life can offer. Settling for the temporal in no way rids us of our inner hunger and thirst for the eternal. Therefore, when we as nonbelievers reject a personal, eternal relationship with our Creator through Jesus Christ, we find ourselves growing increasingly more frustrated and dissatisfied with the beggarly, temporal substitutes for which we have settled.

When we as nonbelievers continually reject God's call to repentance and salvation, God may choose to get our attention by a sign or a warning. Some heed God's signs and warnings. Others, unfortunately, choose to ignore them. Perhaps many of us ignore these signs and warnings because we believe, or at least behave as though we believe, our tomorrows are promised. Scripture teaches that nothing could be farther from the truth (James 4:13-14).

We need to understand that any day could be the day God ends our life, and tragically if we are nonbelievers when that happens, there will be no further opportunities to repent

(Luke 12:16-21). What about us? Has God sent us a sign or a warning? If so, let's heed it and Him for our present and eternal future.

"To all who find their days declining, to all upon whom age is creeping with its infirmities, to all whose strength seems steadily to ebb.... God seems to take our last things, and as it were, pack them up for our journey. These are tokens that you are approaching land. They are signs that the troubles of the sea are almost over." —*Henry Ward Beecher*

Henry Ward Beecher was a prominent, theologically liberal, American Congregationalist clergyman. Beecher was also a social reformer and speaker in the mid to late 19th Century.

If you are a nonbeliever and want to be saved, bow your head and tell God you are truly sorry for your sin and really mean it. Then ask Jesus to come and abide in your heart and save you. There is no magic in our words. God is actually looking at our heart as we pray. Saying the words will not save us. However, if you truly mean the words you are praying with all your heart, Jesus Christ will come into your heart and change your life (Revelation 3:20; 1 John 5:11-12; and Acts 4:10-12).

If you are a believer and want to understand what God is saying to you or teaching you in your circumstance, then earnestly seek Him in prayer for an answer. Even if you do not receive an answer soon, continue to trust Him for He has your best interest at heart, and you will ultimately come to better understand His ways in your life. If this is where you are spiritually, please pray the following:

A Sign, a Warning, and the Undiscerning

Dear heavenly Father, I am seeking to understand what it is You are saying or teaching me in my particular circumstance. You have my attention, and it is the sincere desire of my heart that Your will prevail in my life. Reveal to me Your will for my life; and having done so, help me to obey it. I surrender myself to Your sovereign will to do whatever You deem necessary in my life, which I know, according to Your word, will work to my good and to Your glory. If You choose at this time not to reveal to me what You are doing in my particular circumstance, I accept that as Your sovereign choice. Please strengthen my faith, order my steps in Your Word, and give me an understanding heart and an obedient spirit to wholeheartedly serve You. I ask these things in Jesus' name. Amen.

23

More, Lord, More

An evangelist, preaching to a crowd of enthusiastic people, asked, "How many people here want more faith to better understand how God is directing you? Let me see your hands!" Immediately many hands shot up high into the air. "Then use the faith God has already given you," he preached.

For many years families all over America have enjoyed that classic film, *The Wizard of Oz*. The story chronicles a young girl named Dorothy, who longed for life to be as it was over the rainbow. She traveled far from Kansas to the Land of Oz only to discover what she really longed for in her heart had been available to her all along in Kansas.

If we are not careful and discerning as believers, we too can find ourselves looking and longing for those things God has already made available to us. Paul in his writings to the believers in Ephesus wrote,

> *Wherefore be ye not unwise, but understanding what the will of God is. And be not drunk with wine, wherein is excess; but be filled with the Spirit* (Ephesians 5:17-18).

Contrary to popular belief, being filled with the Spirit of God does not mean we get more of God. We received all of

God we were ever going to get when He entered our hearts and lives in response to our invitation. Being filled with the Holy Spirit means God gets more of us. Therefore, it is not a matter of how much of the Holy Spirit do we have, but rather how much of us does the Holy Spirit have. Being filled with the Holy Spirit means consciously and daily surrendering ourselves totally to His Lordship, and doing as the proverb writer says,

> *Trust in the Lord with all thine heart; and lean not unto thine own understanding. In all thy ways acknowledge Him, and He shall direct thy path* (Proverbs 3:5-6).

Notice how these verses explain that God will indeed direct our path if certain conditions are met first. What are those conditions? We must:

1. Trust Him with all of our heart,

2. Lean not to our own understanding, and

3. In all our ways acknowledge Him.

Regarding acknowledging Him, the Hebrew writer declared,

> *But without faith it is impossible to please Him; for he that cometh to God must believe that He is, and that He is a rewarder of them that diligently seek Him* (Hebrews 11:6).

"He is" in the scripture cited above means the seeker must acknowledge he or she is approaching in faith the one and only true and eternal God. When we come earnestly seeking God in faith and acknowledge Him as the God of the scriptures, He rewards us. How? We get His attention, His presence, and His power as He directs our steps in His service.

When we say in His service, we need to understand there are two types of service. There is directed service, and there is undirected service for the Lord. These two are distinctly different. Luke, the beloved physician, wrote:

> *Now when He* [Jesus] *had left speaking, He said unto Simon, "Launch out into the deep, and let down your nets for a draught." And Simon answering said unto him, "Master, we have toiled all the night, and have taken nothing: nevertheless at thy word I will let down the net". And when they had this done, they inclosed a great multitude of fishes: and their net brake. And they beckoned unto their partners, which were in the other ship, that they should come and help them. And they came, and filled both the ships, so that they began to sink* (Luke 5:4-7).

In Luke's inspired account of this event, Peter readily acknowledged to Jesus they had fished all night without success. Nonetheless, in obedience to Jesus' command to cast down their net again into the same nonproductive waters, Peter and the others complied and cast their net out. The astonished fishermen immediately caught more fish than any one fishing vessel could hold.

So, what made the difference? The difference was directed versus undirected service. When our Lord directs our service, our service produces spiritual fruit. However, when we pursue a course not directed of God, ultimately it produces no spiritual fruit.

Operating outside of God's direction for our lives not only is a fruitless endeavor, but it also brings about a great sense of toil. One way we find ourselves performing undirected service for God is by getting ahead of Him. Our timing is not in sync with God's regarding the activity or ministry in which we find ourselves involved. Notice in Luke's account cited earlier, Jesus directed Peter and the others to do exactly what they had already been doing all night long. His command to cast the same net down into the same waters again was really no different than what these fishermen had been doing for hours. However, when the same net was cast out in the same waters under the divine direction of Jesus Christ, the results were immediately astounding.

So how does this apply to us? From time to time we may find ourselves moving in a ministry direction, which God may one day direct us. The problem is, He has not directed us presently in that particular service. When this happens, the ministry activity we have chosen becomes extremely burdensome to us, and as previously mentioned, produces no real spiritual fruit. Why? It is because we are operating outside of God's perfect timing and will for us. Therefore, God's timing in our lives is of the utmost importance.

What about us? Do we find ourselves asking God for more faith and power to better understand how He is directing us? If so, good for us that we desire His will to prevail in our lives. The encouragement for us is to pray and make sure God is directing our service and learn to wait upon God and not get ahead of Him. If we will do these two things, we can expect God's attention, God's presence, and God's power as He directs our lives in His service. Isaiah wrote,

> *But they that wait upon the LORD shall renew their strength; they shall mount up with wings as eagles; they shall run, and not be weary; and they shall walk, and not faint* (Isaiah 40:31).

"Trees have their seasons at certain times of the year when they bring forth fruit; but a Christian is for all seasons." —*Ralph Brownrigg*

Ralph Brownrigg was born at Ipswich and was Prebendary of Ely, Master of Catharine Hall, Cambridge, Archdeacon of Coventry, and Rector of Barley, in Hertfordshire.

If you are presently struggling to be patient while you wait upon God's direction, and you are tempted to charge off in a ministry direction without first hearing from Him, please remember undirected service eventually becomes extremely burdensome and fruitless. If that is your situation, please pray the following:

Dear heavenly Father, please help me to wait upon You. Your Word says if I do, my spiritual strength will be renewed, and I will be able to run a more effective Christian race. I also understand that any direction I pursue apart from You will ultimately become burdensome to me and spiritually fruitless. Help me to utilize to the fullest for Your glory the faith, gifts, and spiritual power You have already given to me. I humbly ask these things in Jesus' name. Amen.

24

Skin on His Promises

A little five-year-old girl was taught by her mother to kneel each night and pray at her bedside before going to sleep. Her mother would always accompany her daughter in prayer and afterwards tuck the child in for the night.

One particular night as the little girl prayed aloud with her eyes closed, her mother intentionally chose to quietly leave her daughter's side and let the child finish praying alone. Her mother stood silently in the doorway of her daughter's bedroom, watching the little girl pray and hoping her own actions would help her daughter begin adapting to praying on her own.

Sensing something was wrong, the little girl opened her eyes as she continued to pray, but when she discovered her mother was not at her side, she immediately stopped praying. Looking around and spotting her mother standing in the doorway, the little girl pleaded with her mother to return to her side.

Her mother did, and as she again knelt down beside her daughter, the mother asked, "Honey, what's the matter?"

"Don't leave me alone, Mommy. Please!"

"But, honey," the mother comforted, "you're not alone. Jesus is here with you."

"I know, Mommy," sobbed the little girl, "but I want somebody with skin on!"

Jesus promised, "And lo, I am with you always, even unto the end of the world (Matthew 28:20b)." It is our responsibility to put skin on the promises of God. During Jesus' earthly ministry, like us He was subject to the limitations of both time and space. He could only be in one place at a time. However, Jesus foretold of a time to come when the works performed by His followers would be greater than His works (John 14:12).

Greater works than Jesus? How is this possible? Jesus said greater works, not better works. The work performed by followers of Jesus Christ is not greater in power than the miraculous, physical works performed by Jesus; however, the work of His followers is greater in regards to the extent of its spiritual impact upon the world. This is possible because of the indwelling work of the Holy Spirit in the lives of each true follower of Jesus Christ. Therefore, Jesus was foretelling of a time following His ascension when His followers would serve as His spiritual body throughout this world (1 Corinthians 12:12-13).

As members of Jesus Christ's spiritual body, we are His ambassadors in this world (2 Corinthians 5:20). The responsibility of an ambassador is not to represent himself or herself but to represent the one who sent them. Through His spiritual body, Jesus is no longer restricted by the limitations of time and space as He had been in His physical body. Through His spiritual body (the Church), Jesus is simultaneously ministering to the lost, the hurting, the rejected, the needy, the sick, the hungry, the imprisoned, and the destitute in all areas of the globe. Each of us, as followers of Jesus Christ, helps to make up His spiritual body in this world.

Years ago, we moved an elderly great aunt and uncle of ours to our city in order to have them close so we could tend to their needs. It was not long afterwards that we had to put our great uncle in a nursing home due to severe dementia. A couple of years later, our great aunt became extremely ill and needed to be hospitalized. The hospital contacted me and informed me our elderly, ninety-one-year-old aunt was in their emergency room suffering from pneumonia. When I arrived, the hospital emergency staff directed me to her temporary room bordered on each side with a curtain. My aunt was unconscious and unaware of my presence, but her moaning and labored breathing revealed her great discomfort.

The doctor informed me of the severity of her condition, especially at her age. Afterwards, he left me there to sit with my aunt in this temporary room until they could get her stabilized. The doctor informed me that once stabilized, my aunt could be assigned a room in the hospital. Eventually, after two hours or so, they were finally able to get her stabilized and moved to a hospital room.

However, prior to that happening, for those two hours I sat quietly in the temporary room with her. Suddenly, without being lucid, she cried out, "Lord, Lord, I need to spit! Lord, I need to spit!" Her eyes never opened once during this request. I took some moist paper towels and cleaned out her mouth. As soon as I did, my aunt immediately said, "Thank You, Lord." Minutes later and still not lucid, my aunt repeated the request, "Lord, Lord, I need to spit! Lord, I need to spit!" Again, her eyes never opened during this second request. Once more I cleaned out her mouth with moist paper towels and gently rubbed her brow with one of the several clean white towels there in the room. Again, as before, she immediately responded, "Thank You, Lord."

Approximately fifteen or twenty minutes later, she cried out, "Lord, lift my head. Lift my head, Lord." My aunt was laying on her right side, and her head was situated with very little support. This certainly explained why her neck was in such discomfort. I took two clean towels, folded them, lifted her head, and gently placed the towels directly beneath her neck and head. Afterwards, I lowered her neck and head down upon them. I then gently wiped her brow with the same towel as before. The better situating of her head and neck obviously pleased her, because she again responded, "Thank You, Lord." After this, she rested quietly and before long, the hospital staff moved her to a hospital room.

A few days later when my wife and I sat at the kitchen table with our children having our weekly Bible study and devotion, I shared the events of that evening with our children. Hearing these things, our youngest daughter, who was nine at the time, asked, "Daddy, why didn't you tell Aunt G you weren't the Lord?"

In response to her question I smiled and asked her and her three siblings who sat around the table to listen carefully as I read the following passage of scripture.

> *When the Son of man shall come in His glory, and all the holy angels with Him, then shall He sit upon the throne of His glory: And before Him shall be gathered all nations: and He shall separate them one from another, as a shepherd divideth his sheep from the goats: And He shall set the sheep on His right hand, but the goats on the left.*

Then shall the King say unto them on His right hand, Come, ye blessed of My Father, inherit the kingdom prepared for you from the foundation of the world: For I was an hungred, and ye gave Me meat: I was thirsty, and ye gave Me drink: I was a stranger, and ye took Me in: Naked, and ye clothed Me: I was sick, and ye visited Me: I was in prison, and ye came unto Me. Then shall the righteous answer Him, saying, Lord, when saw we Thee an hungred, and fed thee? or thirsty, and gave thee drink? When saw we thee a stranger, and took thee in? or naked, and clothed thee? Or when saw we thee sick, or in prison, and came unto thee? And the King shall answer and say unto them, verily I say unto you, Inasmuch as ye have done it unto one of the least of these my brethren, ye have done it unto me (Matthew 25:31-40).

After reading this passage, I explained to our children that since Jesus Christ has ascended back up into heaven, we are His spiritual body in this world. Therefore, He chooses to have no feet in this world other than our feet to travel to the aide of the sick, hungry, and destitute. He chooses to have no arms in this world other than our arms to hold the sick child or adult who needs to know someone cares. He chooses to have no voice in this world other than our voice to speak kind, comforting words to those who need to hear them the most. I told our children the Lord actually did clean out my aunt's mouth, wipe her brow, and make her head and neck as comfortable as possible; but He chose to do those things through me.

We are the skin God uses in this world to fulfill His promises to minister to those around us. The brethren referred to in this passage of scripture cited above could be viewed as the nation of Israel. It could also be applied to followers of Jesus Christ or anyone destitute and in need of God's love and care. Whether it is a stranger who needs to come to a saving knowledge of Jesus Christ, one who is physically or spiritually sick, an individual who is hungry, or someone who is physically incarcerated, God is ready to touch, heal, and deliver each of these individuals through you and through me.

What about us? Are we available for God's use in His great redemptive work? The Bible tells us in Luke 10:2 we have been called to be co-laborers together with God in this great work of harvesting souls for the kingdom. The Holy Spirit is working through the witness of Christians to minister to both Christians and nonbelievers alike.

You may say, "But I'm not very good at sharing my faith with nonbelievers." Then pray that God will do a work in you that will make you the kind of witness He has called and empowered you to be. Also understand that being a witness for Jesus Christ is not necessarily something we do; being a witness for Jesus Christ is what we are.

> "Evangelism is not a professional job for a few trained men, but is instead the unrelenting responsibility of every person who belongs to the company of Jesus."
> —D. Elton Trueblood

D. Elton Trueblood was a noted 20th Century American author, theologian, Quaker, and former chaplain both to Harvard and Stanford Universities.

If you feel you have not been the best ambassador for the Lord Jesus Christ that you should have been in your home, on your job, at your school, and in your relationships with others, but you desire to be, please tell Him so. Please pray the following:

> Dear heavenly Father, forgive me for not having tried to be the best co-laborer in Your great work of redemption that I could possibly be. I desire to be a better ambassador, a better witness for You, but I need Your help and Your power for this to become a reality in my life. Forgive me and from this day forward empower me for Your holy service. I ask these things in Jesus' name. Amen.

25

Falling and Failure

On one particular night, a restless little three-year-old girl fell out of her bed repeatedly. The first time she fell out of bed that night, the mother—hearing the thud of the girl's body hitting the floor—quickly arose and rushed to the child's room. She comforted her daughter, put the child back into the bed and tucked her in, hoping the child would quickly fall back to sleep as she planted a gentle kiss upon her daughter's brow.

However, within the hour, the mother was again awakened by the sound of another thud as the little girl's body hit the floor a second time. Just as before, the mother rushed to the child's room, picked up her daughter, and placed the child back into bed. Again, as the mother tucked her daughter in, she tenderly planted another kiss on the child's brow.

Approximately thirty minutes later just after the mother had finally dozed off again, she heard the same noise a third time. Fearing her daughter may be hurt, the mother quickly arose and rushed back to the child's room only to find her daughter climbing back up into bed on her own.

The mother tucked her daughter in, softly kissed the child's forehead, and quietly asked, "Sweetheart, do you know why you keep falling out of your bed tonight?"

The little girl looked up at her mother and answered, "I

think, Mommy, it's because I'm staying too close to where I got in."

By sleeping on the edge of her bed, the little girl greatly increased her chances of falling out of it. That same analogy can be applied to our Christian walk. When we fail to grow spiritually beyond the point where we first believed, we greatly increase our chances of falling out of fellowship with our Lord and other believers.

As Christian parents, we work very hard to raise our children to embrace our faith, to become productive members of society, and to be responsible and law-abiding. In short, it can be said that if we do our jobs correctly, we actually raise our children to become independent of us. However, the opposite is true with God. Our heavenly Father raises us, His children, to become more and more dependent on Him. In fact, the more spiritually mature we become, the more reliant on Him we are. The three stages of a Christian's growth could be characterized by the following statements:

1. The baby Christian says, "God has blessed and gifted me; therefore, I can accomplish this myself."
2. The adolescent Christian prays, "God, will You please help me to accomplish this."
3. The adult Christian pleads, "God, it is beyond me to accomplish. You will have to do it through me."

Notice the progression in the statements above as the believer moves from pride to prayer, from a consciousness of self to a consciousness of God, and from a reliance on self to a total reliance on God. Paul, in his first letter to believers in the Corinthian church rebuked them for their carnality.

And I, brethren, could not speak unto you as unto spiritual, but as unto carnal, even as unto babes in Christ. I have fed you with milk, and not with meat: for hitherto ye were not able to bear it, neither yet now are ye able. For ye are yet carnal: for whereas there is among you envying, and strife, and divisions, are ye not carnal, and walk as men? (1 Corinthians 3:1-4)

In this letter to the Corinthian believers, Paul identifies the three kinds of people, spiritually speaking. The first two he identifies in Chapter 2 of this letter. The third one is identified in Chapter 3. According to these inspired words of Paul, there is...

1. The **Natural** man (1 Corinthians 2:14): The natural man is a description of the individual who is unredeemed—spiritually dead. Even if this individual wanted to understand spiritual things, he or she lacks the capacity to do so without the indwelling presence of the Holy Spirit because such things are spiritually discerned.

2. The **Spiritual** man (1 Corinthians 2:15): The spiritual man is the Christian who seeks to walk in fellowship with God and other believers. This individual is not perfect; however, he or she does not hesitate to confess his or her sin before God and sincerely seek the Lord's forgiveness. Worshipping and serving God is the master passion of this individual's life. Such an individual continually seeks the mind of Christ in all matters.

3. The **Carnal** man (1 Corinthians 3:1-4): The carnal man

is the spiritually immature Christian who caters to the appetites of his or her fleshly nature rather than seeking to cultivate intimacy with our Lord. A carnal Christian spends a great deal of time outside of an intimate relationship with God as a result of his or her misplaced priorities.

Paul encouraged carnal believers to grow spiritually and move beyond a diet of spiritual milk to a diet of spiritual meat—beyond spiritual infancy and immaturity, which was characterized by their worldliness, disunity, and squabbling, and become spiritually healthy and mature believers.

"It is because of the hasty and superficial conversation with God that the sense of sin is so weak and that no motives have power to help you to hate and flee from sin as you should." —*Aiden Wilson [A.W.] Tozer*

A.W. Tozer was an American Protestant pastor and preacher, author, Bible conference speaker, and magazine editor.

What about us? Are we spiritual or carnal believers? Are the appetites of our flesh controlling our life and causing us to fall out of fellowship with our Lord? Has sin come between God and us (Isaiah 59:1-2)? Are we in tune with God's will for our lives?

If your walk before our Lord has been carnal, and you desire to walk in fellowship with our Lord, please tell Him so. Just pray the following:

Dear heavenly Father, forgive me for I have been catering to the appetites of my flesh. Admittedly I have failed to be led by Thy Spirit. I know it is Your desire that I be a spiritual Christian, and now that too is my desire as well. I am truly sorry for my carnality and the things I have done in the past which have misrepresented You, and I am asking that You fill me with Your presence and empower me for Your service from this day forward. Please give me a heart and a life that is totally surrendered to You. I ask these things in Jesus' name. Amen.

26

A Lad and His Model Plane

One day a ten-year-old boy who lived in a small town built a model airplane, with the help of his father. The two equipped the plane with a small engine his father had ordered. This made the little boy's airplane the only one of its kind in the little town. One day when the boy was out flying his plane in the park, suddenly a strong wind caught it and drove it off course, causing the boy to lose both the control and the sight of the airplane. The boy searched all evening to find his plane but could not. He was heartbroken.

A couple of weeks later as the boy walked passed the display window of the small town's only hobby shop, he spotted his airplane mounted and on display. The lad raced into the store and begged the owner for his plane, but the storeowner informed the boy he had purchased the plane himself a couple of weeks earlier from a stranger. If the boy wanted it, he would have to purchase it from the store.

The lad went to his father and pleaded with him to purchase the plane, but his father only agreed to make it possible for his son to purchase the plane himself. Following through on the agreement he had made with his son, the next day the father approached several of his neighbors, and all agreed to provide his son with odd jobs so he could earn the money he needed to purchase the plane. Each day for the next two weeks, the boy worked at his neighbors' homes by washing dishes, cleaning floors, raking leaves, dusting and sweeping, washing porches and cars, and doing other work as well. There was something else the lad did each day. He walked by the display window of the hobby shop just to make sure his plane was still there. By the end of the two-week period, the boy had earned enough money to purchase back his plane, and so he did. Upon receiving it from the storeowner, the little boy hugged his plane tightly as he exited the hobby shop saying, "Now you are truly mine because not only did I make you, but I bought you back too."

The story of this lad and his plane is the story of loss and redemption. It is a story of sacrifice, purchase, and the reunion of an owner with his property. When it comes to creation, man stands alongside the entire universe. However, when it comes to redemption, man stands alone, for man alone is the object of God's redemptive plan.

God sent His Son into the world on a search and rescue mission for His precious treasure that had been lost—mankind. Scriptures teach us how God created man in His own image and placed him in the Garden of Eden (Genesis 2:7-8). No one knows how long Adam resided in Eden because the aging process for the first man did not begin until after his fall. It is possible Adam lived hundreds or possibly thousands of years before sinning. Who really knows? What we do know is that Adam did sin, and his sin had a threefold effect:

1. Adam's sin escorted him out of the realm of eternity into the temporal realm of time.

A Lad and His Model Plane

2. Adam's sin wedded him to a second companion. Eve was Adam's first companion, and Adam followed her into sin. Fear became Adam's second companion, and it led him into hiding from the voice of God, and man has been running and hiding from the voice of God every since.

3. Adam's sin passed the dominion over the earth from Adam to Satan and the sin nature to all mankind because in sinning, Adam acted as man's federal head.

Many years ago, modeling clay was a very popular item for thousands of children. Some kids sat for hours playing with this doughy substance endeavoring to create all sorts of animal and human-like creature figures. Imagine yourself having the power to not only fashion the clay into the form of a man-like creature but also possessing the ability to breathe into its nostrils the breath of life.

However, to your dismay when the little clay man stands to his feet, he stubbornly places his hands on his hips and refuses to acknowledge you as his creator. Furthermore, he refuses to listen to you and acknowledge your presence. How would that make you feel?

Imagine how God felt when mankind, His creation, rejected Him. Just because mankind's rejection of God was not met with a speedy, harsh judgment does not mean God overlooked the sin. God neither overlooked nor condoned the offense. He chose instead to over-love it. How? He chose to over-love by sacrificing His Son in our place. Jesus Christ took upon Himself the entire wrath of God against mankind, which was poured out at the cross of Calvary.

Precious stones such as diamonds and rubies have tremendous value because they are so rare. If everyone could stroll out into their yard and dig these stones up, they would be absolutely worthless. One thing is even rarer and therefore more valuable to God than all the precious stones created. In fact, throughout all eternity past and eternity future, God created only one of its kind. This precious, rare item of tremendous value to God is our heart.

God created it, lost it through the sin of Adam, and made provisions to redeem it through the sacrifice of His Son at Calvary. But whether or not our heart is ultimately redeemed is not up to God alone—it is up to us as well. The Bible not only teaches that God in His sovereignty calls us; it also teaches that we have a responsibility to answer His sovereign call. Perhaps this can be said in a simpler way. It is like when we are born, there are three votes cast as to whether or not we will spend eternity in the bliss of God's presence. God votes yes. Satan votes no. You and I have the deciding vote.

> "A world of nice people, content in their own niceness, looking no further, turned away from God, would be just as desperately in need of salvation as a miserable world—and might be even more difficult to save." —*C. S. Lewis*

Lewis was an Irish author and scholar. He is known for his work on medieval literature, Christian apologetics, literary criticism, and fiction. He is best known for his children's series *The Chronicles of Narnia*.

What about you? Does God truly have your heart? Are you absolutely sure that if you died today, you would spend eternity with God in heaven? If not, you can be. Jesus said,

Behold, I stand at the door; and knock: if any man hear

A Lad and His Model Plane

My voice, and open the door; I will come in to him, and will sup with him, and he with Me (Revelation 3:20).

If you want to know beyond any shadow of a doubt that your name is forever sealed in the Lamb's Book of Life (Revelation 20:11-15), please pray the following and by all means mean it with all your heart:

> Dear God in heaven, I come to You confessing I have no assurance that I am truly saved. I desire to have the eternal life, which You offer to all who trust in the sacrifice of Your Son at Calvary. I am now inviting Jesus Christ into my heart. I am sorry for my sin, and I desire to live for You from this day forward. Please take that same power You used to raise Jesus' dead body from that grave and use in my life to make me a new creature in Christ. Thank You for hearing my prayer. Thank You for forgiving me of my sin. Thank You for accepting me into the family of God. In Jesus' name I pray. Amen.

27

A Boy, a Clock, and an Old Man

When I was a boy about twelve years old, I remember accompanying my father on several occasions as he made house and business calls. My father refinished and antiqued furniture for a living. I was always amazed at the expense involved in having furniture repaired, refinished, or antiqued. *A lot of money could be made in this field*, I thought to myself as a young boy. Obviously, others thought so too because many of my father's friends and family tried to persuade him into going into business for himself, but my father was content to work for his employer.

My father's uncle lived directly across the street from us. On one particular evening while I was visiting with him, he asked me to carry his old wooden clock to my father for repair. The clock was about two feet tall and set upon his mantle just over the fireplace in his home. He said to me, "Tell your daddy I will be glad to pay him for fixing it for me."

Time and a few other things had really taken their toll on that old clock. The wood on it was chipped off in several places. It was badly scarred, and the glass facing was completely shattered. In fact, the expense involved in restoring that old clock would have easily exceeded the value of the old clock itself. Nevertheless, my father still took his uncle's old clock to his shop at his place of employment.

A Boy, a Clock, and an Old Man

As time permitted, over the next couple of weeks my father transformed that old rugged, chipped, and scarred, worthless clock into a beautiful, stunning antique with an incredible wood finish, complete with a new glass facing. Of course, the difference in what the old clock had been and what it had become lay in the skill of my father's hands. Having seen my father charge individuals and businesses on several occasions for his work, I knew my great uncle would be incapable of paying the exorbitant amount it would cost for this very fine work.

However, when my father handed me the clock to return to his uncle's house, he gave me specific instructions. My father instructed, "If he asks you how much he owes me, tell him I said he owes me nothing. Just tell him to consider it a gift."

"Yes, sir," I replied as I walked away proudly strutting that magnificent looking clock back across the street to my great uncle's house. He and his family marveled at the sight of their refurbished clock. They could not believe it was the same timepiece. Its transformation exceeded all their expectations.

After several moments of the family's oohs and aahs over the clock, my great uncle pulled me aside and asked, "Son, how much do I owe your daddy?"

"Nothing, sir," I replied as previously instructed. "My daddy said to consider it a gift."

"Oh, no, I have to pay him for this," he insisted.

"But, sir, he said you don't owe him anything!"

He reached down, took my hand, shoved some money into my palm, and said, "Now you tell your daddy I appreciate what he did. Take this money to him because it just wouldn't be right if I didn't pay him."

"Yes, sir," I said, knowing he wasn't giving me a choice. As I walked across the street toward our home, I opened up my hand and there lay in my palm one dollar and a quarter. I handed the money to my father and told him what his uncle had said. He looked at the $1.25 and simply smiled, but he said nothing. In time I came to realize my father had understood from the beginning that his uncle, no matter how well-intentioned, could neither appreciate nor afford the work my father had done on that old rugged, chipped, scarred, and worthless clock.

Like my great uncle, some people find it difficult, if not impossible, to just simply accept God's free gift of grace. God's offer of salvation to us is free, but it was not free for Him. It cost God the Father the life of His Son. The grace God extends to us through the shed blood of His Son Jesus Christ is absolutely priceless; yet in ignorance, many people attempt to pay for it through "works" religions. There are only two kinds of religion—doing and done. A Christian's salvation does not rest in his or her good works but in the finished work of Jesus Christ at Calvary.

Paul wrote to the believers in Ephesus,

For by grace are ye saved through faith; and that not of yourselves: It is the gift of God; not of works, lest any man should boast (Ephesians 2:8-9).

Our faith, which is also God's gift to us, is the vehicle by which we receive salvation, and the source of that salvation is God's grace. In other words, from the source of God's grace through the conduit of faith flows our salvation. This salvation is not a product of anything we have done, can do, or may merit. It is God's gift to us when we take His gift of faith and deposit it in the Person and finished work of Jesus Christ at Calvary.

If we perform righteous acts and deeds in an effort to merit or pay for God's gracious gift of salvation, we insult God. Such actions can be likened to an individual attempting to pay for something utterly priceless with a filthy rag—a rag which is good for nothing except to be discarded (Isaiah 64:6).

Paul wanted the believers in Ephesus to understand there will be absolutely no boasting in heaven because none of the redeemed will be there on his or her own merit. Paul also wanted them to understand that we as Christians perform righteous works not to become saved, but because we are already saved (Ephesians 2:9-10).

When Jesus was asked what is the work that God requires of people in order to earn everlasting life, Jesus replied,

This is the work of God, that ye believe on Him whom He hath sent (John 6:29).

Jesus wanted His listeners to understand that God's salvation does not come from what a person does but in whom a person believes. The only work that is acceptable to God is that we place our faith in His Son Jesus Christ and Christ's finished work at Calvary.

What about us? Have we been attempting to work ourselves into a right relationship with God? If that is what we have been doing, we will never get there. The only way to heaven is by way of Jesus Christ (John 14:6) or by being as righteous as Jesus Christ, and let me assure you no one can measure up to that holy and righteous standard (Romans 3:23).

It is at Calvary's cross we are first introduced to God's amazing grace, but His amazing grace does not end at Calvary's cross. In spite of our sin, God's grace continues to bless our lives with good health, employment and promotions, children who embrace the Savior, and many, many other countless and precious gifts none of us could merit on our own.

> "We believe, that the work of regeneration, conversion, sanctification and faith, is not an act of man's free will and power, but of the mighty, efficacious and irresistible grace of God." —*Charles Spurgeon*

Spurgeon was a British Reformed Baptist pastor who still remains highly influential among Reformed Christians of different denominations

If you are a believer who struggles with resting in the finished work of Jesus Christ, please pray the following:

Dear heavenly Father, thank You for the continual grace and mercy You have shown me as a believer. I know I cannot merit Your favor but somehow, I find myself trying. From this day forward, help me to rest in the finished work of Jesus Christ at Calvary and to understand my works of righteousness are the direct results of Your unmerited favor in my life as a believer. Help me to stop subconsciously and consciously attempting to earn from You what cannot be purchased. I ask these things in Jesus' name. Amen.

28

A Friend on Whom You Can Depend

It was Show-and-Tell day for the fifth graders at Aubrey Elementary. Ten-year-old Timmy was very excited, but if the truth be known, he was a little apprehensive as well. You see, Timmy really loved science so he was eager to show the class his project displaying the effects of magnetism on the growth of plants. He was eager to do so, but he was anxious too because some medicine their family doctor had put him on caused him to have to use the restroom more often than usual.

On this particular day before the 5th graders began filing to the front of the class one by one, presenting and explaining their projects, the teacher, Ms. Barnes at the very start of the class period insisted that as the projects were being presented, she expected every one of her students to give their undivided attention. There would be no talking, no laughing, no note passing, no restroom breaks, and no exceptions. According to Ms. Barnes, every student worked really hard on his/her project and therefore deserved the entire class' complete attention. To ensure every student understood her expectations, Ms. Barnes even made the entire class repeat these rules before any of the projects were presented.

The problem was that Timmy's bladder was about to explode after the 8th kid presented his project presentation.

Timmy nervously rocked back and forth in his seat, wanting so desperately to be excused so he could run to the restroom and relieve his aching bladder. The 9th kid to come forward to present her project was Timmy's best friend Mary. In Timmy's mind, Mary was the best friend in the whole world. She was not only pretty, but she was nice, sweet, tough, and friends with only him. Even the boys wouldn't mess with Mary because she hit harder than most boys.

Mary's project was on fish so she brought tiny ones in a bowl full of water about a gallon in size with five different species of fish. As she was explaining her project to the class, she noticed the distress on Timmy's face. She also noticed he was rocking slowly in his seat, hoping not to be noticed. As Mary stood upfront capturing the entire attention and interest of the class, she suddenly spotted both the pain and embarrassment on Timmy's face as his pants slowly began to moisten around his upper left leg and a very small puddle began to form around his left foot.

Mary suddenly cut her talk short exclaiming, "Well guys, that's all I have, if anyone has any questions, I will try to answer them after class." She rushed forward and deliberately pretended to trip, spilling all the water in the fish bowl into the lap of her friend Timmy. Timmy's trousers were completely soaked and a large puddle of water formed around his left and right shoes. Most of the kids next to Timmy had quickly jumped up and left their seats as the water splashed down upon Timmy and puddled beneath his seat.

"Mary, sweetie, what happened?" came the voice of Ms. Barnes as she called out to the young lady who had fallen to her knees.

Mary looked up at her friend Timmy, winked, and with a warm smile whispered, "It's okay, Timmy, I got this."

A Friend on Whom You Can Depend

Looking back at Ms. Barnes, Mary exclaimed, "I'm so sorry, Ms. Barnes, I must have tripped over my own feet. I'll clean it up."

"No child," Ms. Barnes replied. "I'll have the custodian come and clean this mess up. Oh my goodness, looks like we'll just have to continue with the last two projects tomorrow.

Then turning her attention to Timmy, Ms. Barnes remarked, "Oh, Timmy, I am so sorry that your pants got soaked. Please help Mary collect those fish, and I'll call your parents and have them come and get you. Okay?"

"Yes, ma'am," Timmy answered as he turned to Mary and whispered. "You saved me."

Mary smiled. "That's what friends are for."

I am confident that if asked to define what it means to be a friend, several definitions would be articulated. However, a common theme in most of those responses would be descriptions such as: 1) someone who truly loves and cares about me, 2) someone I can depend on, and 3) someone who always tries to have my back.

What about the friends we had when we were still nonbelievers? Many of these friends no longer walk with us. Why is that? It could be because in the minds of our former friends the two of us no longer have anything in common, at least not enough in common to remain friends. In fact, after our coming to faith in Jesus Christ, we may have noticed these same former friends conveniently always have something else to do or some other place they have to be when responding to our invitations.

Even family members at times find themselves at odds—husband against wife, parents against children, and siblings against siblings. Many will confess they have friends they are closer to than their own family members, but at times even these close friends let us down. However, the scriptures declare:

A man of too many friends comes to ruin, But there is a friend who sticks closer than a brother (Proverbs 18:24 NASB).

Proverbs 18:24 informs us that in our lives we may have two sets of friends. On the one hand, we may have those who call themselves our friends simply because of what they believe we can do for them. The prodigal son had these kinds of friends (Luke 15:11-32). They partied with him because he was picking up the tab. The problem was that when the prodigal son exhausted all his resources and found himself destitute, he quickly discovered not one of those so-called friends hung around to help him.

On the other hand, there are those friends who genuinely love and care about us and our welfare. Such friends may even be closer to us than our very own family members, or as it's said in the scriptures—they stick closer to us than an actual blood brother. They can be counted on to have our best interests at heart, and they always seek to have our backs—just like Mary in our story who was looking out for Timmy or like Jonathan who was closer to David than David's own brothers.

There is, however, a Friend above all friends we can always count on, even when the closest of our friends let us down. His name is Jesus. Jesus Christ is our closest Friend

A Friend on Whom You Can Depend

and has our eternal best interest at heart. During His earthly ministry, He was known by many as a Friend to sinners and publicans (Luke 7:34). For those who have truly invited Him into their hearts, Jesus calls us His friends (John 15:15). As believers, our Friend Jesus has promised to be with us even until the end of the age (Matthew 28:20) and to never leave or forsake us (Hebrews 13:5). What family member anywhere can make such promises to us? Truly Jesus is that Friend that sticks closer than any brother could.

> "Let those be thy choicest companions who have made Christ their chief companion." —*Thomas Brooks*

Thomas Brooks (1608–1680) was an English non-conformist Puritan preacher and author.

If you have failed to seek and cultivate intimacy with our God through His Son Jesus, who is the friend above all friends, and now you desire that relationship and intimacy, please tell Him. Simply pray the following:

> Dear God in heaven, forgive me for seeking one relationship after another that ultimately fails me in one way or the other. Help me to put my eyes on You and seek the ultimate of all possible relationships in You through the sacrifice of Your Son Jesus Christ at Calvary. I confess to You that I am a sinner, and I am begging You to wash me and cleanse me from all my unrighteousness. I invite Your Son Jesus into my heart right now, and I beg You to take that same power which You used to raise Jesus' dead body from the

grave. Please use that same power in my life to make me into a new creature that serves and honors You with all my heart and life from this day forth. I ask this in Jesus' name. Amen.

29

A Question of Compassion

A church missed its pastor of twenty-five years after he lost his long battle with a terminal illness. As a result, the church formed a pastoral search committee in hopes of determining who their next pastor would be. The committee contacted a well-known seminary and asked the school to submit recommendations for their consideration. The seminary responded with the names of two outstanding candidates—John and Tom. The president of the seminary spoke very highly of both young men. According to him, both John and Tom were graduating at the end of the semester, and their academic records were comparable. The search committee reviewed the files of both candidates and was highly impressed with each. Both John and Tom were interviewed and both interviews went extremely well. Afterwards, both candidates were invited to deliver a Sunday morning sermon to the church.

John was the first one scheduled to preach. On the Sunday morning he arrived, he stood before the assembly, opened his Bible to Luke 16 and preached a stirring message entitled Lazarus and the Rich Man. He delivered a very powerful sermon, and the congregation was very pleased.

The following Sunday morning, Tom arrived to preach a sermon. Tom stood before the assembly, opened his Bible to the Luke 16, and also preached a stirring message entitled Lazarus and the Rich Man. He too delivered a very powerful sermon, and the congregation was very pleased.

After much prayer and discussion, the search committee recommended to the church that John, not Tom, be their next pastor. The church approved the recommendation and the candidates were notified. One of the church's members later asked the wise old deacon who chaired the search committee how the committee was able to recommend one candidate over the other.

"They were practically equal in every way," the member commented.

The old deacon replied, "Well, as you said yourself, it was a very difficult decision to make with both men being so equally matched in almost every way. But, with God's help and guidance, we were finally able to make our choice based on the sermons each of them preached."

"But how? They both preached the same message from the same scripture, and both sermons were outstanding," the puzzled member quickly pointed out.

"Well, this is true, but you see," the wise old deacon remarked, "when Tom preached about Lazarus and the rich man, he seemed pleased the old rich man finally got what he deserved. However, when John preached the same message, he was noticeably saddened by the fact that the rich man wound up in Hades, even though he deserved to be there. I guess you could say our recommendation for our Church's next pastor boiled down to a question of compassion."

A Question of Compassion

John became the church's next pastor because the compassion in his heart was evident in his words and witnessed in his ministry. Someone has appropriately said, "Preachers should never preach about hell unless they do it with a broken heart because hell is a terrible place."

Our Lord is a God of compassion. The Prophet Jeremiah declared the primary reason the wicked and disobedient are not cut down in the midst of their sin and rebellion is because of God's great love, mercy, and compassion, which never fail and are new every morning (Lamentations 3:22-23a).

Like the candidate John in the story, it is absolutely essential we who are followers of Jesus Christ show compassion toward others if God is to be glorified in our lives. Showing love and compassion to friends and family, while refusing to show it to others whom we dislike or who dislike us, is not particularly noteworthy. Jesus declared,

> *For if ye love them which love you, what thank have ye? For sinners also love those that love them. And if ye do good to them which do good to you, what thank have ye? For sinners also do even the same. And if ye lend to them of whom ye hope to receive, what thank have ye? for sinners also lend to sinners, to receive as much again. But love ye your enemies, and do good, and lend, hoping for nothing again; and your reward shall be great, and ye shall be the children of the Highest; for He is kind unto the unthankful and to the evil. Be ye therefore merciful, as your Father also is merciful* (Luke 6:32-36).

Jesus was saying if we are God's children, then our actions should reveal we are truly God's children. God is loving, gracious, compassionate, and generous, and so should we, His children, be as well. Those whose hearts have been touched by the power of God's love will return good for evil and exhibit love and compassion by attempting to meet specific needs of friends and foe. Failure to do this is to deprive the world of its opportunity to see God's love and compassion at work in us. The Apostle John wrote,

> *But whoso hath this world's good, and seeth his brother have need, and shutteth up his bowels of compassion from him, how dwelleth the love of God in him* (1 John 3:17).

If God's love and compassion are flowing in our lives, then His love and compassion should be flowing through our lives as well to meet the physical, emotional, and spiritual needs of those around us. The more we behave like our heavenly Father's children, the more others around us are persuaded God is dwelling within us. It is not enough to pray for God's blessings on others if we are not willing to be the instrument He uses to do the blessing. James wrote,

> *If a brother or sister be naked and destitute of daily food, and one of you say unto them, depart in peace, be ye warmed and filled; notwithstanding ye give them not those things which are needful to the body; what doth it profit* (James 2:15-16).

Kind words do not fill empty stomachs. Pats on the back will not clothe the naked. Professing a love lacking in compassion is no more genuine than professing a faith that lacks obedience. We have no greater example of love and compassion than what is seen in the actions of our loving heavenly Father in the sending of His only begotten Son on a search and rescue mission to redeem us from our fallen state (John 3:16).

A Question of Compassion

"Compassion costs. It is easy enough to argue, criticize, and condemn, but redemption is costly, and comfort draws from the deep. Brains can argue, but it takes a heart to comfort." —*Samuel Chadwick*

Samuel Chadwick, an English Pastor, preacher, and writer, became a lay pastor at Stacksteads in Lancashire at the age of twenty-one. He was performing mission work in the South Yorkshire coal fields in 1912 when he returned to Cliff College and was formally appointed principal in 1913. Chadwick authored among other books *The Way to Pentecost* and *The Call to Christian Perfection*.

What about you? Is there really compassion in your heart for your foes, or is it reserved only for your friends and family? Is the compassion in your heart evident in both your words and your life? If not and you want it to be, please pray the following:

Dear heavenly Father, give me a compassionate heart for others and not just for those whom I like and who like me. I recognize I have freely received compassion from You many times over, so I am sincerely asking You to help me be compassionate to everyone, including my foes from this day forward. I ask these things in Jesus' name. Amen.

30

Strawberries and Squash

Several years ago, my wife's employer sent her to Washington D.C. for a week long training seminar. Of course, this meant I was left behind with our four small children to be chief cook and bottle washer for the entire week. Although I love to cook, Doretha, my wife, usually did the honors because our kids, when they were small, never acquired a taste for my kitchen experiments.

The first evening I decided to prepare something I felt would be both healthy and good tasting—stewed yellow squash—yum, yum! Given that the kids were not at all enthused Dad was cooking, I wanted this squash to taste extra special. *Something sweet*, I thought, *would surely make squash more appealing*, and so I promptly dumped several cups of strawberries into the pot. When I served the colorful dish that evening, the kids looked at it dubiously. After one bite, India, our ten-year-old daughter, said, "Daddy, this stuff is awful!"

I said, "Listen, sweetie, it's supposed to be good for you," and then I took my first bite. She was right, even though that concoction may have been good for us, it was indeed awful. We all sat there with contorted faces and reluctantly finished our healthy meal.

After that evening whenever I cooked, our kids were

quick to bow their heads; however, I am confident they were not saying grace—they were simply asking God for mercy.

There comes a time in each of our lives as Christians when God sets before us an unpleasant meal and a bitter cup. He did no less for His Son. Jesus understood that unless He drank from the bitter cup His Father set before Him, there would be no redemption for mankind and all would be eternally doomed (Matthew 26:39-42). We too must understand that unless we are willing to eat and drink from the unpleasant dish and bitter cup God sets before us, our spiritual growth is impeded, and our availability to be used of God to impact the lives of others is limited.

In Matthew's gospel account, James and John, accompanied by their mother, approached Jesus. Their mother asked if each of her sons could sit immediately to Jesus' right and left when He came into His kingdom (Matthew 20:21-22). Jesus said to them, "You do not know what you are asking. Are you able to drink the cup that I am about to drink?" Without knowing what was in the cup, the two confidently answered, "We are able."

After Christ's ascension, James and John, along with the other followers of Christ, soon discovered what was in this bitter cup Jesus said Christians would indeed drink from (Matthew 20:23).

Following His resurrection and just prior to His ascension, Jesus served His church an appetizer called the Great Commission. It proved to be an appetizer His Jewish followers were hesitant to partake of. Why? Their deep-rooted prejudice against Gentiles made these Jewish believers reluctant to share the gospel message with anyone who was not a Jew.

Peter was even called on the carpet and required to explain himself for sharing the gospel message with Cornelius, a Gentile and Roman centurion, along with Cornelius' family and friends who were present in his house (Acts 10:19-48; 11:1-17). In His commission to the Church, Jesus commanded that we go forth and teach all nations and baptize all who believe (Matthew 28:19-20).

Jesus said the Holy Spirit would empower Christians to be His witnesses, sharing the gospel message in Jerusalem, Judea, Samaria, and the uttermost parts of the world (Acts 1:8). Is that what these Jewish believers did? No, at least not initially when they discovered it meant sharing the gospel message with people they despised.

Next the Lord allowed these Jewish believers to be served an unpleasant entrée and bitter cup called persecution. James was killed by the sword, and Stephen was stoned to death. In 64 A.D., Nero began a blood bath in Rome by falsely accusing Christians of setting the fire that burned nearly three-quarters of the city. Persecution left a bitter taste in the mouth of Christians, but spiritually speaking it proved to be beneficial for the Gentiles. Why? It is because persecution scattered the Jewish Christians abroad, and as they scattered, these Jewish Christians shared the gospel message wherever they went.

The gospel was not only shared with other Jews but with people in Samaria (Acts 8:14-17) where the people were part Jewish. It was even shared with Gentiles in faraway lands (Acts 10, 13-23). Although bitter to the taste, persecution prompted many Jews in the early church to fulfill the Great Commission.

What is it going to take for some of us as Christians to begin sharing our faith with those around us? Will it take a spiritually unpleasant meal or bitter cup? Suffering cannot be all bad when it serves to make us spiritually stronger and more obedient to God.

Sometimes we need to be reminded that as Christians we are God's spiritual flashlights. When our circumstances become dark, God enables us to shine our brightest. Flashlights were never designed for sunlight. Flashlights were designed for darkness that people may find their way. Jesus Christ is the Way (John 14:6), and our commission is to shine our light in the presence of those who stumble in spiritual darkness in order that they may find their way to our Lord (Matthew 5:16).

The late Corrie ten Boom, author of *The Hiding Place*, once said when a bird flies for pleasure, it flies with (in the direction of) the wind. However, when that bird is threatened, it turns and faces the wind that it might gain altitude and rise higher.

Each day God calls us as believers to crawl upon His altar and become living sacrifices (Romans 12:1) that He may be glorified in our lives. This means when God lights a fire on the altar beneath us, we will experience great discomfort. However, we are encouraged by the scriptures to stay on the altar because these unpleasant experiences serve to make us into the individuals God wants us to become.

However, if and when you and I crawl off the altar because of our great discomfort or when we avoid His altars altogether, we miss out on the wonderful opportunity to be the salt and light Jesus spoke of in Matthew 5:13-16. Corrie ten Boom said soaring with the wind can be pleasurable, but Christians who have learned to face the wind become stronger and soar higher.

> "You will have no test of faith that will not fit you to be a blessing if you are obedient to the Lord. I never had a trial but when I got out of the deep river I found some poor pilgrim on the bank that I was able to help by that very experience." —*Albert Benjamin Simpson*

Albert Benjamin Simpson was a Canadian author, theologian, preacher, and founder of The Christian and Missionary Alliance (C&MA), an evangelical Protestant denomination with an emphasis on global evangelism.

What will you do? Will you live for pleasure or will you seek God's power? In which direction are you willing to fly?

When God prepares a table before us, let's ask Him for strength to be willing to eat of that unpleasant meal and to drink from that bitter cup. It will make us spiritually healthy and more effective as His witnesses in this world. If you desire for God to be glorified in your life by becoming the individual He has called and empowered you to be, please pray the following prayer:

> Dear Father, forgive me for failing to see Your hand in each of my circumstances. I believe Your Word when it says all things work together for good to them who love You, to them who are called according to Your

purpose. However, I confess when my circumstances have been unpleasant, I have not responded in faith, and my actions failed to demonstrate an understanding of what I profess to believe. Forgive me for misrepresenting You before others during my times of testing and temptations. Help me from this day forward to pursue Your wisdom and Your power in my life, not that I may be glorified in my trials, but that You may be glorified in my life—even during my trials. I surrender every area of my heart and life to Your lordship from this day forward. Please give me a submissive spirit and a continual hunger and thirst for Your righteousness. I ask these things in Jesus' name. Amen.

About the Authors

VANDERBILT BRABSON III was born in Knoxville, Tennessee, and graduated from the University of Tennessee. Vanderbilt's wife, Doretha, whom he wed in April 1981, is deceased. They had two daughters (India and Van'esha) and two sons (Vanderbilt IV and Joshua).

A conference speaker and writer, Vanderbilt is one of the featured writers in *Ordinary People* magazine.

Vanderbilt wrote two fiction books, entitled *The Gatekeeper* and *Beyond the Lies* and is presently releasing for publication this non-fiction book, *If the Shoe Fits*, co-authored with his brother Frederick E. Brabson Sr., in the winter of 2019.

FREDERICK E. BRABSON SR., a graduate of Johnson University Bible College, has more than thirty years of preaching, Bible teaching, and conference speaking experience. He has served as Senior Pastor of the New Covenant Baptist Church (National Baptist and Southern Baptist) for twenty-five years. Frederick has been married to his wife, Delores, for 41 years, and they have two sons, Frederick II and Nicholas.

He is also founder of the Relevant Word Ministries, the television outreach ministries of the church. The Relevant Word Ministries television broadcasts are viewed weekly on Saturdays and twice on Sundays on CTN and daily on KRBB on a number of cable, satellite, and wireless channels reaching hundreds of thousands of homes and businesses in East Tennessee and the surrounding areas. Pastor Brabson has also served as the Director of Evangelism for Knox County Association of Baptists, Southern Baptist Convention (SBC), and Tennessee Baptist Convention (TBC). He is a well-known conference speaker, sharing the podium with various speakers such as Henry Blackaby (author of *Experiencing God*).